AN ANTHOLOGY
OF ENGLISH POETRY:
DRYDEN TO BLAKE

AN ANTHOLOGY
OF
ENGLISH POETRY:
DRYDEN TO BLAKE

Compiled by
KATHLEEN CAMPBELL

Granger Index Reprint Series

BOOKS FOR LIBRARIES PRESS
FREEPORT, NEW YORK

First Published 1930
Reprinted 1971

INTERNATIONAL STANDARD BOOK NUMBER
0-8369-6297-4

LIBRARY OF CONGRESS CATALOG CARD NUMBER
75-168777

PRINTED IN THE UNITED STATES OF AMERICA
BY
NEW WORLD BOOK MANUFACTURING CO., INC.
HALLANDALE, FLORIDA 33009

INDEX OF FIRST LINES

	PAGE
Ae fond kiss, and then we sever!	245
Ah me! full sorely is my heart forlorn . . .	143
All in the Downs the fleet was moor'd . . .	65
As Rochfoucault his maxims drew	45
As swift as Time put round the Glass . . .	96
Awake! Aeolian lyre	159
Behold what marks of majesty she brings . .	32
Blest Leaf! whose aromatic Gales dispense . .	128
But are you sure the news is true? . . .	209
But what are these to great Atossa's mind? . .	85
But why so far excursive?	102
By these presents be it known	165
Come, O Thou traveller unknown	131
Condemn'd to Hope's delusive mine . . .	138
Confess'd from yonder slow-extinguished clouds .	102
Cruelty has a human heart	250
Dear Cloe, how blubber'd is that pretty face? .	41
Dear Dick, howe'er it comes into his Head .	41
Distracted with Care	38
Doeg, though without knowing how, or why .	27
Enough of Self—that darling, luscious theme .	194
False though she be to me and Love . . .	50
Farewell, too little and too lately known . .	13
Forth goes the woodman	207
Friend of the moss-grown Spire	180
From dearth to plenty and from death to life .	208
From White's and Will's.	54
Guide me, O thou great Jehovah	164
Hark how all the Welkin rings	129
Hark, my soul! it is the Lord	203

5

INDEX OF FIRST LINES

	PAGE
Here, a sheer hulk .	210
Here end my Chains	43
Here lies the Lyric	68
Hope humbly then, with trembling pinions soar	83
How sleep the Brave	166
I love the windows of thy Grace	51
If ought of Oaten stop, or Pastoral song .	170
In full-blown dignity, see Wolsey stand	134
In such a Night, when every louder wind	37
In these deep solitudes	79
In vain to me the smiling Mornings shine	153
In yonder grave a Druid lies .	167
Is there, for honest poverty	233
It was a' for our rightfu' King	241
Jesus, Lord, in Pity hear us	130
John Gilpin was a citizen	195
Last May a braw wooer .	238
Little Lamb, who made thee?	247
Lords, knights and squires, the num'rous band	39
Love divine, all Loves excelling	132
Love seeketh not itself to please	250
Mary, I want a lyre with other strings	203
Mistaken fair, lay Sherlock by	95
My love is like a red red rose	244
My noble, lovely little Peggy .	42
My Time, O ye Muses .	93
No! not for Those of Women born	93
O Mortal Man, who livest here by Toil .	107
O ruddier than the Cherry	68
O, synge untoe mie roundelaie	212
O that those lips had language!	202
O thou by Nature taught	168
O Thou, that sit'st upon a throne	172
O thou! whatever title suit thee	227
O, wert thou in the cauld blast,	244
O, winter, ruler of the inverted year	206

INDEX OF FIRST LINES

	PAGE
O ye wha are sae guid yoursel	231
Of all the girls that are so smart	91
Of old, when Scarron his companions invited	181
Oft I've implored the gods in vain	161
Our God, our help in ages past	53
Our Panther, though like these she changed her head	29
Phyllida, that lov'd to dream	64
Piping down the valleys wild	246
Pomposo (insolent and loud)	191
Pope has the talent well to speak	44
Scenes that soothed or charmed me young	204
Scots wha hae wi' Wallace bled	240
Shock's fate I mourn	63
Should auld acquaintance be forgot	242
Shut, shut the door, good John!	86
Silent Nymph, with curious Eye	122
Soft slept the sea within its silver bed	190
Sweet Auburn! loveliest village of the plain	183
Temperance, exercise and air	127
The curfew tolls the knell of parting day	153
The First, who, from his native soil remov'd	192
The Jews, a headstrong, moody, murmuring race	16
The keener tempests come	105
The Merchant, to secure his Treasure	40
The spacious Firmament on high	50
The sun descending in the west	247
The Village Life, and every care that reigns	214
There was three Kings into the east	236
This motley piece to you I send	96
Thou fair-hair'd angel of the evening	246
Thou youngest virgin-daughter of the skies	33
Thus solitary, and in pensive guise	104
Tiger! Tiger! burning bright	249
'Tis true—then why should I repine	43
To me, who in their lays the shepherds call	172
To see a World in a grain of sand	250
To thee, fair freedom! I retire	143

	PAGE
Toll for the brave	200
'Twas on a lofty vase's side	157
Unless with my Amanda blest	101
We are a Garden wall'd around . . .	52
Wee, sleekit, cow'rin', tim'rous beastie . .	234
Well then, the promised hour is come at last .	14
Whan I sleep I dream	242
What a rout do you make	166
What dire offence from am'rous causes springs .	69
When biting Boreas, fell and dour . . .	235
When chapman billies leave the street . .	222
When Delia on the plain appears . . .	133
When the sheep are in the fauld . . .	211
While shepherds watch'd their Flocks by Night .	36
Why are those tears?	66
Ye flowery banks o' bonnie Doon . . .	243
Ye golden Lamps of Heav'n, farewell . .	127
Ye shepherds so cheerful and gay . . .	139
Ye Warwickshire lads, and ye lasses . .	162
Yes, I'll maintain what you have often said .	61
Yes, I'm in love, I feel it now . . .	152
You charmed me not with that fair face . .	35
Young Colin Clout, a Lad of peerless Meed .	54
Youth's the Season made for Joys . . .	68

INDEX OF AUTHORS

	PAGE
Joseph Addison, 1672-1719	50
Mark Akenside, 1721-1770	172
Lady Anne Barnard, 1750-1825	211
William Blake, 1757-1827	246
Isaac Hawkins Browne, 1705-1760	128
Robert Burns, 1759-1796	222
John Byrom, 1692-1763	93
Henry Carey, d. 1743	91
Thomas Chatterton, 1752-1770	212
Charles Churchill, 1731-1764	191
William Collins, 1721-1759	166
William Congreve, 1670-1729	50
William Cowper, 1731-1800	195
George Crabbe, 1754-1832	214
Charles Dibdin, 1745-1814	210
Philip Doddridge, 1702-1751	127
John Dryden, 1631-1700	13
John Dyer, 1700-1757	122
Anne Finch, Lady Winchelsea, 1661-1720	37
David Garrick, 1717-1779	162
John Gay, 1685-1732	54
Oliver Goldsmith, 1728-1774	181
George Granville, Earl of Lansdowne, 1667-1735	43
Thomas Gray, 1716-1771	153
Matthew Green, 1696-1737	96
Frances Greville, dates unknown, fl. 1750	161
Samuel Johnson, 1709-1784	134
George Lyttleton, Lord Lyttleton, 1709-1773	133
Sir James Marriott, ? 1730-1803	190
William Mickle, 1735-1788	209
Ambrose Philips, 1675-1749	54
Alexander Pope, 1688-1744	69
Matthew Prior, 1664-1721	39
William Shenstone, 1714-1763	139
Christopher Smart, 1722-1771	172
Philip Stanhope, Earl of Chesterfield, 1694-1773	95
Jonathan Swift, 1667-1745	43

INDEX OF AUTHORS

	PAGE
Nahum Tate, 1657–1715	36
James Thomson, 1700–1748	101
Horace Walpole, Earl of Orford, 1717–1797	165
William Walsh, 1663–1708	38
Joseph Warton, 1722–1800	180
Isaac Watts, 1674–1748	51
Charles Wesley, 1707–1788	129
Samuel Wesley, the younger, 1691–1739	93
William Whitehead, 1715–1785	152
William Williams, 1717–1791	164

Key to Absalom and Achitophel

Abethdin	Lord Chancellor
Absalom	Duke of Monmouth
Achitophel	Lord Shaftesbury
Agag	Sir Edmund Godfrey
Balaam	Earl of Huntingdon
Caleb	Lord Grey
Corah	Titus Oates
David	King Charles II
Doeg	Elkanah Settle
Egypt	France
Gath	Brussels
Hebron	Scotland
Ishbosheth	Richard Cromwell
Israel	England
Jebusites	Roman Catholics
Jerusalem	London
Jews	English
Jonas	Sir William Jones
Jordan	Dover
Nadab	Lord Howard of Escrick
Og	Thomas Shadwell
Pharaoh	King of France
Saul	Oliver Cromwell
Shimei	Sheriff Bethel
Zimri	Duke of Buckingham

JOHN DRYDEN (1631-1700)
TO THE MEMORY OF MR. OLDHAM

FAREWELL, too little and too lately known,
Whom I began to think and call my own:
For sure our souls were near allied, and thine
Cast in the same poetic mould with mine.
One common note on either lyre did strike,
And knaves and fools we both abhorred alike.
To the same goal did both our studies drive:
The last set out the soonest did arrive.
Thus Nisus fell upon the slippery place,
Whilst his young friend performed and won the race.
O early ripe! to thy abundant store
What could advancing age have added more?
It might (what Nature never gives the young)
Have taught the numbers of thy native tongue.
But Satire needs not those, and wit will shine
Through the harsh cadence of a rugged line.
A noble error, and but seldom made,
When poets are by too much force betrayed.
Thy gen'rous fruits, though gathered ere their prime,
Still shewed a quickness; and maturing Time
But mellows what we write to the dull sweets of rhyme.
Once more, hail, and farewell! farewell, thou young
But ah! too short, Marcellus of our tongue!
Thy brows with ivy and with laurels bound;
But fate and gloomy night encompass thee around.

TO MY DEAR FRIEND, MR. CONGREVE

WELL then, the promis'd hour is come at last;
The present age of wit obscures the past:
Strong were our Sires, and as they fought they writ,
Conqu'ring with force of arms and dint of wit:
Theirs was the giant race before the flood;
And thus, when Charles return'd, our Empire stood.
Like Janus, he the stubborn soil manur'd,
With rules of husbandry the rankness cur'd:
Tam'd us to manners, when the stage was rude,
And boistrous English wit with art indu'd.
Our age was cultivated thus at length,
But what we gained in skill we lost in strength.
Our builders were with want of genius curs'd;
The second temple was not like the first;
Till you, the best Vitruvius, come at length,
Our beauties equal, but excel our strength.
Firm Doric pillars found your solid base,
The fair Corinthian crowns the higher space;
Thus all below is strength, and all above is grace.
In easy dialogue is Fletcher's praise:
He mov'd the mind, but had no power to raise.
Great Johnson did by strength of judgement please,
Yet, doubling Fletcher's force, he wants his ease.
In diff'ring talents both adorn'd their age,
One for the study, t'other for the stage.
But both to Congreve justly shall submit,
One match'd in judgement, both o'er-match'd in wit.
In him all beauties of this age we see,
Etherege his courtship, Southern's purity,
The satire, wit, and strength of manly Wycherly.
All this in blooming youth you have achiev'd;
Nor are your foil'd contemporaries griev'd;
So much the sweetness of your manners move,
We cannot envy you, because we love.
Fabius might joy in Scipio, when he saw
A beardless Consul made against the law,

And join his suffrage to the votes of Rome,
Though he with Hannibal was overcome.
Thus old Romano bow'd to Raphael's fame,
And scholar to the youth he taught, became.
 O that your brows my laurel had sustain'd,
Well had I been depos'd, if you had reign'd!
The Father had descended for the Son,
For only you are lineal to the Throne.
Thus, when the State one Edward did depose,
A greater Edward in his room arose :
But now, not I, but Poetry is curs'd ;
For Tom the second reigns like Tom the first.
But let 'em not mistake my Patron's part
Nor call his charity their own desert.
Yet this I prophesy ; Thou shalt be seen,
(Tho' with some short parenthesis between :)
High on the throne of wit ; and, seated there,
Nor mine (that's little) but thy laurel wear ;
Thy first attempt an early promise made ;
That early promise this has more than paid.
So bold, yet so judiciously you dare,
That your least praise, is to be regular.
Time, place, and action may with pains be wrought,
But genius must be born, and never can be
 taught.
This is your portion, this your native store :
Heav'n, that but once was prodigal before,
To Shakespear gave as much ; she could not give him
 more.
 Maintain your post : that's all the fame you need ;
For 'tis impossible you should proceed.
Already I am worn with cares and age,
And just abandoning the ungrateful stage :
Unprofitably kept at Heav'n's expense,
I live a rent-charge on his providence :
But you, whom ev'ry Muse and grace adorn,
Whom I forsee to better fortune born,
Be kind to my remains ; and Oh defend,
Against your judgement, your departed friend !

Let not th' insulting foe my fame pursue ;
But shade those laurels which descend to you :
And take for tribute what these lines express ;
You merit more ; nor could my love do less.

From ABSALOM AND ACHITOPHEL, Part I

THE Jews, a headstrong, moody, murmuring race,
As ever tried th' extent and stretch of grace ;
God's pampered people, whom, debauched with ease
No king could govern, nor no God could please :
(Gods they had tried of every shape and size
That god smiths could produce, or priests devise :)
These Adam-wits, too fortunately free,
Began to dream they wanted liberty ;
And when no rule, no precedent was found
Of men by laws less circumscribed and bound,
They led their wild desires to woods and caves
And thought that all but savages were slaves.
They who, when Saul was dead, without a blow
Made foolish Ishbosheth the crown forego ;
Who banished David did from Hebron bring,
And with a general shout proclaimed him king ;
Those very Jews who at their very best,
Their humour more than loyalty exprest,
Now wondered why so long they had obeyed
An idol monarch, which their hand had made ;
Thought they might ruin him they could create,
Or melt him to that golden calf, a state.
But these were random bolts ; no formed design
Nor interest made the factious crowd to join :
The sober part of Israel, free from stain,
Well knew the value of a peaceful reign ;
And, looking backward with a wise affright,
Saw seams of wounds, dishonest to the sight ;
In contemplation of whose ugly scars
They cursed the memory of civil wars.
The moderate sort of men thus qualified,
Inclined the balance to the better side ;

And David's mildness managed it so well
The bad found no occasion to rebel.
But when to sin our biased nature leans,
The careful devil is still at hand with means,
And providently pimps for ill desires ;
The good old cause, revived, a plot requires.
Plots, true or false, are necessary things
To raise up commonwealths and ruin kings.
  Th' inhabitants of old Jerusalem
Were Jebusites ; the town so called from them.
But when the chosen people grew more strong,
The rightful cause at length became the wrong ;
And every loss the men of Jebus bore,
They still were thought God's enemies the more.
Thus worn or weakened, well or ill content,
Submit they must to David's government :
Impoverished and deprived of all command,
Their taxes doubled as they lost their land :
And, what was harder yet to flesh and blood,
Their gods disgraced, and burnt like common wood.
This set the heathen priesthood in a flame ;
For priests of all religions are the same.
Of whatso'er descent their godhead be,
Stock, stone, or other homely pedigree,
In his defence his servants are as bold
As if he had been born of beaten gold.
The Jewish rabbins, though their enemies,
In this conclude them honest men and wise ;
For 'twas their duty, all the learned think,
T' espouse his cause by whom they eat and drink.
From hence began that plot, the nation's curse,
Bad in itself, but represented worse ;
Raised in extremes, and in extremes decried ;
With oaths affirmed, with dying vows denied ;
Not weighed or winnowed by the multitude,
But swallowed in the mass unchewed and crude.
Some truth there was, but dashed and brewed with lies,
To please the fools, and puzzle all the wise :

Succeeding times did equal folly call,
Believing nothing, or believing all.
Th' Egyptian rites the Jebusites embraced,
Where gods were recommended by their taste.
Such savoury deities must needs be good
As served at once for worship and for food.
By force they could not introduce these gods :
For ten to one in former days was odds.
So fraud was used (the sacrificer's trade) ;
Fools are more hard to conquer than persuade.
Their busy teachers mingled with the Jews,
And raked for converts ev'n the court and stews ;
Which Hebrew priests the more unkindly took,
Because the fleece accompanies the flock.
Some thought they God's anointed meant to slay
By guns, invented since full many a day ;
Our author swears it not ; but who can know
How far the devil and Jebusites may go.
This plot, which failed for want of common sense,
Had yet a deep and dangerous consequence
For as, when raging fevers boil the blood,
The standing lake soon floats into a flood,
And every hostile humour, which before
Slept quiet in its channels, bubbles o'er ;
So several factions, from this first ferment,
Work up to foam, and threat the government.
Some by their friends, more by themselves, thought wise,
Opposed the power to which they could not rise ;
Some had in courts been great, and thrown from thence,
Like fiends, were hardened in impenitence :
Some, by their monarch's fatal mercy, grown
From pardoned rebels, kinsmen to the throne,
Were raised in power and public office high ;
Strong bands, if bands ungrateful men could tie.
 Of these the false Achitophel was first,
A name to all succeeding ages curst :
For close designs and crooked counsels fit,
Sagacious, bold, and turbulent of wit ;

Restless, unfixed in principles and place,
In power unpleased, impatient of disgrace ;
A fiery soul, which working out its way,
Fretted the pigmy body to decay,
And o'er-informed the tenement of clay.
A daring pilot in extremity ;
Pleased with the danger, when the waves went high,
He sought the storms ; but, for a calm unfit,
Would steer too nigh the sands to boast his wit.
Great wits are sure to madness near allied,
And thin partitions do their bounds divide ;
Else, why should he, with wealth and honour blest,
Refuse his age the needful hours of rest ?
Punish a body which he could not please,
Bankrupt of life, yet prodigal of ease ?
And all to leave what with his toil he won
To that unfeathered, two legged thing, a son :
Got while his soul did huddled notions try,
And born a shapeless lump, like anarchy.
In friendship false, implacable in hate,
Resolved to ruin or to rule the state.
To compass this the triple bond he broke,
The pillars of the public safety shook,
And fitted Israel for a foreign yoke ;
Then seized with fear, yet still affecting fame,
Usurped a patriot's all-atoning name.
So easy still it proves, in factious times,
With public zeal to cancel private crimes :
How safe is treason and how sacred ill,
Where none can sin against the people's will !
Where crowds can wink, and no offence be known,
Since in another's guilt they find their own.
  Yet fame deserved, no enemy can grudge ;
The statesman we abhor, but praise the judge.
In Israel's courts ne'er sat an Abethdin
With more discerning eyes, or hands more clean ;
Unbribed, unsought, the wretched to redress,
Swift of despatch, and easy of access.

Oh! had he been content to serve the crown
With virtues only proper to the gown;
Or had the rankness of the soil been freed
From cockle that oppressed the noble seed;
David for him his tuneful harp had strung,
And heaven had wanted one immortal song.
But wild ambition loves to slide, not stand,
And fortune's ice prefers to virtue's land.
Achitophel, grown weary to possess
A lawful fame, and lazy happiness,
Disdained the golden fruit to gather free,
And lent the crowd his arm to shake the tree.
Now, manifest of crimes contrived long since,
He stood at bold defiance with his prince;
Held up the buckler of the people's cause
Against the crown, and skulked behind the laws.
The wished occasion of the plot he takes,
Some circumstances finds, but more he makes;
By buzzing emissaries fills the ears
Of listening crowds with jealousies and fears
Of arbitrary counsels brought to light,
And proves the king himself a Jebusite.
Weak arguments! which yet he knew full well
Were strong with people easy to rebel:
For, governed by the moon, the giddy Jews
Tread the same track when she the prime renews;
And once in twenty years, their scribes record,
By natural instinct they change their lord.
Achitophel still wants a chief, and none
Was found so fit as warlike Absalom:
Not that he wished his greatness to create,
(For politicians neither love nor hate)
But, for he knew his title not allowed,
Would keep him still depending on the crowd:
That kingly power, thus ebbing out, might be
Drawn to the dregs of a democracy.
Him he attempts with studied arts to please,
And sheds his venom in such words as these:

" Auspicious prince, at whose nativity
Some royal planet ruled the southern sky,
Thy longing country's darling and desire,
Their cloudy pillar and their guardian fire ;
Their second Moses, whose extended wand
Divides the seas and shows the promised land,
Whose dawning day in every distant age,
Has exercised the sacred prophet's rage :
The people's prayer, the glad diviner's theme,
The young men's vision, and the old men's dream !
Thee, Saviour, thee the nation's vows confess,
And, never satisfied with seeing, bless :
Swift unbespoken pomps thy steps proclaim,
And stammering babes are taught to lisp thy name ;
How long wilt thou the general joy detain,
Starve and defraud the people of thy reign ;
Content ingloriously to pass thy days
Like one of virtue's fools that feeds on praise ;
Till thy fresh glories, which now shine so bright,
Grow stale and tarnish with our daily sight ?
Believe me, royal youth, thy fruit must be
Or gathered ripe, or rot upon the tree.
Heaven has to all allotted, soon or late,
Some lucky revolution of their fate ;
Whose motions, if we watch and guide with skill,
(For human good depends on human will,)
Our fortune rolls as from a smooth descent,
And from the first impression, takes the bent ;
But, if unseized, she glides away like wind,
And leaves repenting folly far behind.
Now, now she meets you with a glorious prize,
And spreads her locks before you as she flies.
Had thus old David, from whose loins you spring,
Not dared, when fortune called him, to be king,
At Gath an exile he might still remain,
And heaven's anointing oil had been in vain.
Let his successful youth your hopes engage,
But shun th' example of declining age ;

Behold him setting in his western skies,
The shadows lengthening as the vapours rise.
He is not now as when, on Jordan's sand,
The joyful people thronged to see him land,
Covering the beach, and blackening all the strand ;
But, like the prince of angels, from his height
Comes tumbling downward with diminished light,
Betrayed by one poor plot to public scorn ;
(Our only blessing since his cursed return ;)
Those heaps of people, which one sheaf did bind,
Blown off, and scattered by a puff of wind.
What strength can he to your designs oppose,
Naked of friends, and round beset with foes ?
If Pharaoh's doubtful succour he should use,
A foreign aid would more incense the Jews ;
Proud Egypt would dissembled friendship bring,
Foment the war, but not support the king ;
Nor would the royal party e'er unite
With Pharaoh's arms t' assist the Jebusite ;
Or if they should, their interest soon would break,
And, with such odious aid make David weak.
All sorts of men, by my successful arts,
Abhorring kings, estrange their altered hearts
From David's rule ; and 'tis the general cry,
Religion, commonwealth, and liberty.
If you, as champion of the public good,
Add to their arms a chief of royal blood,
What may not Israel hope, and what applause
Might such a general gain by such a cause ?
Not barren praise alone, that gaudy flower,
Fair only to the sight, but solid power :
And nobler is a limited command,
Given by the love of all your native land,
Than a successive title, long and dark,
Drawn from the mouldy rolls of Noah's ark."

    What cannot praise effect in mighty minds,
When flattery soothes, and when ambition blinds ?
Desire of power, on earth a vicious weed,
Yet, sprung from high, is of celestial seed :

In God 'tis glory; and when men aspire,
'Tis but a spark too much of heavenly fire.
Th' ambitious youth, too covetous of fame,
Too full of angels' metal in his frame,
Unwarily was led from virtue's ways,
Made drunk with honour, and debauched with praise.
Half loth and half consenting to the ill,
(For loyal blood within him struggled still)
He thus replied :—" And what pretence have I
To take up arms for public liberty ?
My father governs with unquestioned right,
The faith's defender, and mankind's delight;
Good, gracious, just, observant of the laws,
And heaven by wonders has espoused his cause.
Whom has he wronged in all his peaceful reign ?
Who sues for justice to his throne in vain ?
What millions has he pardoned of his foes,
Whom just revenge did to his wrath expose ?
Mild, easy, humble, studious of our good,
Inclined to mercy, and averse from blood.
If mildness ill with stubborn Israel suit,
His crime is God's beloved attribute.
What could he gain his people to betray,
Or change his right for arbitrary sway ?
Let haughty Pharaoh curse with such a reign
His fruitful Nile, and yoke a servile train.
If David's rule Jerusalem displease,
The dog-star heats their brains to this disease.
Why then should I, encouraging the bad,
Turn rebel, and run popularly mad ?
Were he a tyrant, who by lawless might
Oppressed the Jews, and raised the Jebusite,
Well might I mourn ; but nature's holy bands
Would curb my spirits and restrain my hands:
The people might assert their liberty;
But what was right in them, were crime in me,
His favour leaves me nothing to require,
Prevents my wishes, and outruns desire :

What more can I expect while David lives?
All but his kingly diadem he gives:
And that "—but there he paused; then, sighing,
    said,—
" Is justly destined for a worthier head.
For when my father from his toils shall rest,
And late augment the number of the blest,
His lawful issue shall the throne ascend,
Or the collateral line, where that shall end.
His brother, though oppressed with vulgar spite,
Yet dauntless, and secure of native right,
Of every royal virtue stands possest,
Still dear to all the bravest and the best:
His courage foes, his friends his truth proclaim,
His loyalty the king, the world his fame:
His mercy e'en the offending crowd will find,
For sure he comes of a forgiving kind.
Why should I then repine at heaven's decree,
Which gives me no pretence to royalty?
Yet, oh that fate, propitiously inclined,
Had raised my birth, or had debased my mind;
To my large soul not all her treasure lent,
And then betrayed it to a mean descent.
I find, I find my mounting spirits bold,
And David's part disdains my mother's mould.
Why am I scanted by a niggard birth?
My soul disclaims the kindred of her earth,
And, made for empire, whispers me within,
Desire of greatness is a godlike sin." . . .
Such were the tools; but a whole hydra more
Remains, of sprouting heads, too long to score.
Some of their chiefs were princes of the land:
In the first rank of these did Zimri stand;
A man so various, that he seemed to be
Not one, but all mankind's epitome:
Stiff in opinions, always in the wrong,
Was everything by starts, and nothing long;
But, in the course of one revolving moon,
Was chemist, fiddler, statesman, and buffoon:

Then all for women, painting, rhyming, drinking,
Besides ten thousand freaks that died in thinking.
Blest madman ! who could every hour employ
With something new to wish or to enjoy !
Railing and praising were his usual themes,
And both (to show his judgment) in extremes ;
So over violent, or over civil,
That every man, with him, was God or devil.
In squandering wealth was his peculiar art ;
Nothing went unrewarded, but desert.
Beggar'd by fools, whom still he found too late ;
He had his jest, and they had his estate.
He laughed himself from court ; then sought relief
By forming parties, but could ne'er be chief :
For, spite of him, the weight of business fell
On Absalom and wise Achitophel :
Thus, wicked but in will, of means bereft,
He left not faction, but of that was left.
   Titles and names 'twere tedious to rehearse
Of lords below the dignity of verse :
Wits, warriors, commonwealth's-men, were the best,
Kind husbands, and mere nobles, all the rest.
And therefore, in the name of dulness, be
The well-hung Balaam and cold Caleb free ;
And canting Nadab let oblivion damn,
Who made new porridge for the paschal lamb.
Let friendship's holy band some names assure.
Some their own worth, and some let scorn secure.
Nor shall the rascal rabble here have place,
Whom kings no titles gave, and God no grace :
Not bull-faced Jonas, who could statutes draw
To mean rebellion, and make treason law.
But he, though bad, is followed by a worse,
The wretch who heaven's anointed dared to curse,
Shimei, whose youth did early promise bring
Of zeal to God, and hatred to his king ;
Did wisely from expensive sins refrain,
And never broke the sabbath but for gain ;

Nor was he ever known an oath to vent,
Of curse, unless against the government.
Thus heaping wealth, by the most ready way
Among the Jews, which was to cheat and pray ;
The city, to reward his pious hate
Against his master, chose him magistrate.
His hand a vase of justice did uphold ;
His neck was loaded with a chain of gold.
During his office, treason was no crime ;
The sons of Belial had a glorious time :
For Shimei, though not prodigal of pelf,
Yet loved his wicked neighbour as himself.
When two or three were gathered to declaim
Against the monarch of Jerusalem,
Shimei was always in the midst of them ;
And if they cursed the king when he was by,
Would rather curse than break good company.
If any durst his factious friends accuse,
He packed a jury of dissenting Jews,
Whose fellow-feeling in the godly cause
Would free the suffering saint from human laws :
For laws are only made to punish those
Who serve the king, and to protect his foes.
If any leisure time he had from power,
(Because 'tis sin to misemploy an hour,)
His business was, by writing, to persuade
That kings were useless, and a clog to trade :
And, that his noble style he might refine,
No Rechabite more shunned the fumes of wine,
Chaste were his cellars, and his shrieval board
The grossness of a city-feast abhorred :
His cooks, with long disuse, their trade forgot ;
Cool was his kitchen, though his brains were hot.
Such frugal virtue malice may accuse,
But sure 'twas necessary to the Jews :
For towns, once burnt, such magistrates require,
As dare not tempt God's providence by fire.
With spiritual food he fed his servants well,
But free from flesh that made the Jews rebel ;

And Moses' laws he held in more account,
For forty days of fasting in the mount.

From PART II

DOEG, though without knowing how or why,
Made still a blundering kind of melody,
Spurred boldly on, and dashed through thick and thin,
Through sense and nonsense, never out nor in;
Free from all meaning, whether good or bad,
And, in one word, heroically mad:
He was too warm on picking-work to dwell,
But faggoted his notions as they fell,
And if they rhymed and rattled all was well
Spiteful he is not, though he wrote a satire,
For still there goes some thinking to ill-nature:
He needs no more than birds and beasts to think,
All his occasions are to eat and drink:
If he call rogue and rascal from a garret,
He means you no more mischief than a parrot:
The words for friend and foe alike were made,
To fetter 'em in verse is all his trade.
For almonds he'll cry whore to his own mother;
And call young Absalom king David's brother.
Let him be gallows free by my consent,
And nothing suffer, since he nothing meant:
Hanging supposes human soul and reason,
This animal's below committing treason:
Shall he be hanged who never could rebel?
That's a preferment for Achitophel.
Railing in other men may be a crime,
But ought to pass for mere instinct in him:
Instinct he follows, and no further knows,
For to write verse with him is to *transprose*.
'Twere pity treason at his door to lay,
Who makes heaven's gate a lock to its own key.
Let him rail on; let his invective muse
Have four-and-twenty letters to abuse,

Which if he jumbles to one line of sense,
Indict him of a capital offence.
In fireworks give him leave to vent his spite,
Those are the only serpents he can write:
The height of his ambition is, we know,
But to be master of a puppet-show;
On that one stage his works may yet appear,
And a month's harvest keeps him all the year.

   Now stop your noses, readers, all and some,
For here's a tun of midnight-work to come,
Og, from a treason tavern rolling home.
Round as a globe, and liquored every chink,
Goodly and great he sails behind his link;
With all this bulk, there's nothing lost in Og,
For every inch that is not fool is rogue:
A monstrous mass of foul corrupted matter,
As all the devils had spued to make the batter.
When wine has given him courage to blaspheme,
He curses God; but God before cursed him:
And if man could have reason, none has more,
That made his paunch so rich and him so poor.
With wealth he was not trusted, for Heaven knew
What 'twas of old to pamper up a Jew:
To what would he on quail and pheasant swell,
That e'en on tripe and carrion could rebel?
But though Heaven made him poor, with reverence speaking,
He never was a poet of God's making:
The midwife laid her hand on his thick skull,
With this prophetic blessing—Be thou dull;
Drink, swear, and roar, forbear no lewd delight
Fit for thy bulk; do anything but write:
Thou art of lasting make, like thoughtless men:
A strong nativity—but for the pen!
Eat opium, mingle arsenic in thy drink,
Still thou mayest live, avoiding pen and ink.
I see, I see 'tis counsel given in vain,
For treason botched in rhyme will be thy bane:

Rhyme is the rock on which thou art to wreck;
'Tis fatal to thy fame and to thy neck.
Why should thy metre good king David blast?
A psalm of his will surely be thy last.
Dar'st thou presume in verse to meet thy foes,
Thou, whom the penny pamphlet foiled in prose?
Doeg, whom God for mankind's mirth has made,
O'ertops thy talent in thy very trade:
Doeg, to thee thy paintings are so coarse,
A poet is, though he's the poet's horse.
A double noose thou on thy neck dost pull,
For writing treason, and for writing dull:
To die for faction is a common evil,
But to be hanged for nonsense is the devil.
Hadst thou the glories of thy king exprest,
Thy praises had been satire at the best;
But thou in clumsy verse, unlicked, unpointed,
Hast shamefully defied the Lord's anointed.
I will not rake the dunghill of thy crimes,
For who would read thy life that reads thy rhymes?
But of king David's foes be this the doom,
May all be like the young man Absalom;
And for my foes, may this their blessing be,
To talk like Doeg, and to write like thee.

From THE HIND AND THE PANTHER, Part I

   Our Panther, [1]though like these she changed her head,
Yet, as the mistress of a monarch's bed,
Her front erect with majesty she bore,
The crosier wielded, and the mitre wore.
Her upper part, of decent discipline,
Showed affectation of an ancient line;
And fathers, councils, church, and churches' head
Were on her reverend phylacteries read:
But what disgraced and disavowed the rest
Was Calvin's brand that stigmatized the beast.

[1] The Church of England.

Thus, like a creature of a double kind,
In her own labyrinth she lives confined.
To foreign lands no sound of her is come,
Humbly content to be despised at home.
Such is her faith, where good cannot be had,
At least she leaves the refuse of the bad :
Nice in her choice of ill, though not of best,
And least deformed, because reformed the least.
In doubtful points betwixt her differing friends,
Where one for substance one for sign contends,
Their contradicting terms she strives to join,
Sign shall be substance, substance shall be sign.
A real presence all her sons allow,
And yet 'tis flat idolatry to bow,
Because the Godhead's there they know not
  how.
Her novices are taught that bread and wine
Are but the visible and outward sign,
Received by those who in communion join ;
But th' inward grace, or the thing signified,
His blood and body, who to save us died ;
The faithful this thing signified receive :
What is't those faithful then partake or leave ?
For what is signified and understood
Is, by her own confession, flesh and blood :
Then, by the same acknowledgment, we know
They take the sign, and take the substance too.
The literal sense is hard to flesh and blood,
But nonsense never can be understood.
  Fierce to her foes, yet fears her force to try,
Because she wants innate authority :
For how can she constrain them to obey,
Who has herself cast off the lawful sway ?
Rebellion equals all, and those who toil
In common theft, will share the common spoil.
Let her produce the title and the right
Against her old superiors first to fight ;
If she reform by text, e'en that's as plain
For her own rebels to reform again.

As long as words a different sense will bear,
And each may be his own interpreter,
Our airy faith will no foundation find;
The word's a weathercock for every wind:
The Bear,[1] the Fox,[2] the Wolf,[3] by turns prevail;
The most in power supplies the present gale.
The wretched Panther cries aloud for aid
To church and councils, whom she first betrayed;
No help from Fathers or tradition's train;
Those ancient guides she taught us to disdain,
And by that Scripture, which she once abused
To reformation, stands herself accused.
What bills for breach of laws can she prefer,
Expounding which she owns herself may err?
And, after all her winding ways are tried,
If doubts arise she slips herself aside,
And leaves the private conscience for the guide:
If then that conscience set th' offender free,
It bars her claim to church authority.
How can she censure, or what crime pretend,
But Scripture may be construed to defend?
E'en those whom for rebellion she transmits
To civil power, her doctrine first acquits;
Because no disobedience can ensue
Where no submission to a judge is due;
Each judging for himself, by her consent,
Whom thus absolved she sends to punishment.
Suppose the magistrate revenge her cause,
'Tis only for transgressing human laws,
How answering to its end a church is made,
Whose power is but to counsel and persuade?
O solid rock, on which secure she stands!
Eternal house, not built with mortal hands!
O sure defence against th' infernal gate,
A patent during pleasure of the state!
  Thus is the Panther neither loved nor feared,
A mere mock queen of a divided herd;

[1] Independents.   [2] Arians.   [3] Presbyterians.

Whom soon by lawful power she might control,
Herself a part submitted to the whole:
Then, as the moon, who first receives the light
By which she makes our nether regions bright,
So might she shine, reflecting from afar
The rays she borrowed from a better star;
Big with the beams which from her mother flow,
And reigning o'er the rising tides below:
Now mixing with a savage crowd she goes,
And meanly flatters her inveterate foes.
Ruled while she rules, and losing every hour
Her wretched remnants of precarious power.

From PART II

BEHOLD what marks of majesty she [1] brings,
Richer than ancient heirs of eastern kings:
Her right hand holds the sceptre and the keys,
To show whom she commands, and who obeys;
With these to bind, or set the sinner free,
With that t' assert spiritual royalty.
One in herself, not rent by schism, but sound,
Entire, one solid shining diamond;
Not sparkles shattered into sects, like you;
One is the church, and must be, to be true:
One central principle of unity,
As undivided, so from errors free,
As one in faith, so one in sanctity.
Thus she, and none but she, th' insulting rage
Of heretics opposed from age to age:
Still when the giant-brood invades her throne,
She stoops from heaven, and meets 'em half-way down,
And with paternal thunder vindicates her crown.
But like Egyptian sorcerers you stand,
And vainly lift aloft your magic wand,
To sweep away the swarms of vermin from the land:
You could, like them, with like infernal force,
Produce the plague, but not arrest the course.

[1] The Roman Catholic Church.

But when the boils and botches, with disgrace
And public scandal, sat upon the face,
Themselves attacked, the Magi strove no more,
They saw God's finger, and their fate deplore ;
Themselves they could not cure of the dishonest sore.
Thus one, thus pure, behold her largely spread,
Like the fair ocean from her mother-bed ;
From east to west triumphantly she rides,
All shores are watered by her wealthy tides :
The gospel-sound, diffused from pole to pole,
Where winds can carry, and where waves can roll ;
The self-same doctrine of the sacred page
Conveyed to every clime in every age.

AN ODE

TO THE PIOUS MEMORY OF THE ACCOMPLISHED YOUNG LADY, MRS. ANNE KILLIGREW

THOU youngest virgin-daughter of the skies,
Made in the last promotion of the blest ;
Whose palms, new-plucked from Paradise,
In spreading branches more sublimely rise,
Rich with immortal green above the rest :
Whether, adopted to some neighbouring star,
Thou rollest above us, in the wandering race,
 Or, in procession fixed and regular,
 Movest with the heaven's majestic pace ;
 Or, called to more superior bliss,
Thou tread'st, with seraphims, the vast abyss :
Whatever happy region is thy place,
Cease thy celestial song a little space ;
Thou wilt have time enough for hymns divine,
 Since heaven's eternal year is thine.
Hear then a mortal muse thy praise rehearse,
  In no ignoble verse.
But such as thy own voice did practise here,
When thy first-fruits of poesy were given ;
To make thyself a welcome inmate there :
  While yet a young probationer,
  And candidate of heaven. . . .

A.E.P.

May we presume to say, that at thy birth
New joy was sprung in heaven, as well as here on earth.
   For sure the milder planets did combine
   On thy auspicious horoscope to shine,
   And e'en the most malicious were in trine.
   Thy brother-angels at thy birth
     Strung each his lyre, and tuned it high,
     That all the people of the sky
   Might know a poetess was born on earth.
    And then, if ever, mortal ears
   Had heard the music of the spheres.
   And if no clustering swarm of bees
   On thy sweet mouth distilled their golden dew,
     'Twas that such vulgar miracles
     Heaven had not leisure to renew:
   For all thy blest fraternity of love
Solemnized there thy birth, and kept thy holiday above.

   O gracious God! how far have we
Profaned thy heavenly gift of poesy!
Made prostitute and profligate the Muse,
Debased to each obscene and impious use,
Whose harmony was first ordained above
For tongues of angels, and for hymns of love!
O wretched we! why were we hurried down
   This lubrique and adulterate age,
  (Nay, added fat pollutions of our own,)
     T' increase the steaming ordures of the stage?
What can we say t' excuse our second fall?
Let this thy vestal, heaven, atone for all:
Her Arethusian stream remains unsoiled,
Unmixed with foreign filth, and undefiled;
Her wit has more than man, her innocence a child.

    Art she had none, yet wanted none,
    For nature did that want supply;
    So rich in treasures of her own,
    She might our boasted stores defy:
Such noble vigour did her verse adorn,
That it seemed borrowed where 'twas only born.

Her morals, too, were in her bosom bred;
  By great examples daily fed,
What in the best of books, her father's life, she read.
And to be read herself she need not fear;
Each test, and every light, her Muse will bear,
Though Epictetus with his lamp were there.
E'en love (for love sometimes her Muse exprest)
Was but a lambent flame which played about her breast,
Light as the vapours of a morning dream;
So cold herself, while she such warmth exprest,
'Twas Cupid bathing in Diana's stream. . . .

  When in mid-air the golden trump shall sound,
    To raise the nations under ground;
    When in the valley of Jehoshaphat,
  The judging God shall close the book of fate;
    And there the last assizes keep,
    For those who wake and those who sleep;
    When rattling bones together fly
    From the four corners of the sky;
When sinews o'er the skeletons are spread,
Those clothed with flesh, and life inspires the dead;
The sacred poets first shall hear the sound,
And foremost from the tomb shall bound,
For they are covered with the lightest ground;
And straight, with inborn vigour, on the wing,
Like mounting larks, to the new morning sing.
There thou, sweet saint! before the choir shalt go,
As harbinger of heaven, the way to show,
The way which thou so well has learnt below.

SONG

  You charmed me not with that fair face,
    Though it was all divine:
  To be another's is the grace
    That makes me wish you mine.
  The gods and fortune take their part,
    Who, like young monarchs, fight

And boldly dare invade that heart,
   Which is another's right.
First, mad with hope, we undertake
   To pull up every bar;
But, once possessed, we faintly make
   A dull defensive war.
Now, every friend is turned a foe,
   In hope to get our store:
And passion makes us coward grow,
   Which made us brave before.

NAHUM TATE (1657–1715)
SONG OF THE ANGELS AT THE NATIVITY OF OUR BLESSED SAVIOUR

WHILE Shepherds watch'd their Flocks by Night
   all seated on the Ground,
The Angel of the Lord came down,
   and Glory shone around.
" Fear not," said he, (for mighty Dread
   had seiz'd their troubled Mind)
" Glad Tidings of great Joy I bring
   to you and all Mankind;
" To you, in *David's* Town this Day
   is born of *David's* Line,
" The Saviour, who is Christ the Lord;
   and this shall be the Sign:
" The heav'nly Babe you there shall find
   to human view display'd,
" All meanly wrapt in swathing Bands,
   and in a Manger laid."
Thus spake the Seraph, and forthwith
   appear'd a shining Throng
Of Angels praising God, and thus
   addrest their joyful Song;
' All Glory be to God on high,
   and to the Earth be peace;
" Goodwill, henceforth, from Heav'n to Men,
   begin and never cease."

ANNE FINCH, LADY WINCHELSEA
(1661–1720)
A NOCTURNAL REVERIE

IN such a *Night*, when every louder Wind
Is to its distant Cavern safe confin'd ;
And only gentle *Zephyr* fans his Wings,
And lonely *Philomel*, still waking, sings ;
Or from some Tree, fam'd for the *Owl's* delight,
She, hollowing clear, directs the Wand'rer right :
In such a *Night*, when passing Clouds give place,
Or thinly veil the Heav'ns mysterious Face ;
When in some River, overhung with Green,
The waving Moon and trembling Leaves are seen ;
When freshen'd Grass now bears itself upright,
And makes cool Banks to pleasing Rest invite,
Whence springs the *Woodbine*, and the *Bramble*-Rose,
And where the sleepy *Cowslip* shelter'd grows ;
Whilst now a paler hue the *Foxglove* takes,
Yet chequers still with Red the dusky brakes :
When scatter'd *Glow-worms*, but in Twilight fine,
Shew trivial Beauties watch their hour to shine ;
Whilst *Salisb'ry* stands the Test of every Light,
In perfect Charms, and perfect Virtue bright :
When Odours, which declin'd repelling Day,
Through temp'rate Air uninterrupted stray ;
When darken'd Groves their softest Shadows wear,
And falling Waters we distinctly hear ;
When thro' the Gloom more venerable shows
Some ancient Fabric, awful in Repose,
While Sunburnt Hills their swarthy Looks conceal,
And swelling Haycocks thicken up the Vale :
When the loos'd *Horse* now, as his Pasture leads,
Comes slowly grazing thro' th' adjoining Meads,
Whose stealing Pace, and lengthen'd Shade we fear,
Till torn-up Forage in his Teeth we hear :
When nibbling *Sheep* at large pursue their Food,
And unmolested Kine rechew the Cud ;

When *Curlews* cry beneath the Village-walls,
And to her straggling Brood the *Partridge* calls;
Their short-liv'd Jubilee the Creatures keep,
Which but endures, whilst Tyrant-*Man* does sleep:
When a sedate Content the Spirit feels,
And no fierce Light disturbs, whilst it reveals;
But silent Musings urge the Mind to seek
Something, too high for Syllables to speak;
Till the free Soul to a compos'dness charm'd,
Finding the Elements of Rage disarm'd,
O'er all below a solemn Quiet grown,
Joys in th' inferior World, and thinks it like her Own:
In such a *Night* let Me abroad remain,
Till Morning breaks, and All's confus'd again;
Our Cares, our Toils, our Clamours are renew'd,
Or Pleasures, seldom reach'd, again pursu'd.

WILLIAM WALSH (1663–1708)

THE DESPAIRING LOVER

DISTRACTED with Care,
For *Phillis* the Fair;
Since nothing could move her,
Poor *Damon*, her Lover,
Resolves in Despair
No longer to languish,
Nor bear so much Anguish;
But, mad with his Love,
To a Precipice goes;
Where, a Leap from above
Would soon finish his Woes.

When in Rage he came there,
Beholding how steep
The Sides did appear,
And the Bottom how deep;
His Torments projecting,
And sadly reflecting,

That a Lover forsaken
A new Love may get;
But a Neck when once broken,
Can never be set;
And, that he could die
Whenever he would;
But, that he could live
But as long as he could:
How grievous soever
The Torment might grow,
He scorn'd to endeavour
To finish it so.
But Bold, Unconcern'd
At Thoughts of the Pain,
He calmly return'd
To his Cottage again.

MATTHEW PRIOR (1664-1721)
TO A CHILD OF QUALITY
Five Years Old, the Author Forty. 1704.

LORDS, knights, and squires, the num'rous band,
  That wear the fair miss *Mary's* fetters,
Were summon'd by her high command,
  To show their passions by their letters.

My pen amongst the rest I took,
  Lest those bright eyes that cannot read
Should dart their kindling fires, and look,
  The power they have to be obey'd.

Nor quality, nor reputation,
  Forbid me yet my flame to tell;
Dear five years old befriends my passion,
  And I may write till she can spell.

For while she makes her silk-worms beds,
  With all the tender things I swear,
Whilst all the house my passion reads,
  In papers round her baby's hair;

She may receive and own my flame,
    For tho' the strictest prudes should know it,
She'll pass for a most virtuous dame,
    And I for an unhappy poet.

Then too, alas ! when she shall tear
    The lines some younger rival sends,
She'll give me leave to write I fear,
    And we shall still continue friends.

For as our diff'rent ages move,
    'Tis so ordained, would fate but mend it,
That I shall be past making love,
    When she begins to comprehend it.

AN ODE

THE Merchant, to secure his Treasure,
    Conveys it in a borrow'd Name :
Euphelia serves to grace my Measure ;
    But *Cloe* is my real Flame.

My softest Verse, my darling Lyre,
    Upon *Euphelia's* Toilet lay ;
When *Cloe* noted her Desire,
    That I should sing, that I should play.

My Lyre I tune, my Voice I raise,
    But with my Numbers mix my Sighs :
And, whilst I sing *Euphelia's* Praise,
    I fix my Soul on *Cloe's* Eyes.

Fair *Cloe* blush'd, *Euphelia* frown'd ;
    I sung and gaz'd, I play'd and trembl'd :
And *Venus* to the *Loves* around
    Remark'd, how ill we all dissembl'd.

HORACE, LIB. I, EPIST. IX, IMITATED
TO THE RIGHT HONORABLE MR. HARLEY

DEAR DICK, howe'er it comes into his Head,
Believes, as firmly as He does his Creed,
That You and I, Sir, are extremely great;
Tho' I plain Mat, you *Minister of State*.
One Word from Me, without all doubt, He says,
Would fix his Fortune in some little Place.
Thus better than My self, it seems, He knows,
How far my Interest with my Patron goes;
And answering all Objections I can make,
Still plunges deeper in his dear Mistake.
From this wild Fancy, Sir, there may proceed
One wilder yet, which I foresee, and dread;
That I, in Fact, a real Interest have,
Which to my own Advantage I would save,
And, with the usual Courtier's Trick, intend
To serve My self, forgetful of my Friend.
  To shun this Censure, I all Shame lay by;
And make my Reason with his Will comply;
Hoping, for my Excuse, 'twill be confessed
That of two Evils I have chose the least.
So, Sir, with this Epistolary Scroll,
Receive the Partner of my inmost Soul:
Him you will find in Letters, and in Laws
Not unexpert, firm to his Country's Cause,
Warm in the Glorious Interest You pursue,
And, in one Word, a Good Man and a True.

A BETTER ANSWER

DEAR CLOE, how blubber'd is that pretty Face?
  Thy Cheek all on Fire, and Thy Hair all uncurl'd
Prithee quit this Caprice; and (as Old Falstaff says)
  Let Us e'en talk a little like Folks of This World.

How can'st Thou presume, Thou hast leave to destroy
　　The Beauties, which VENUS but lent to Thy keeping?
Those Looks were design'd to inspire Love and Joy:
　　More ordinary Eyes may serve People for weeping.

To be vexed at a Trifle or two that I writ,
　　Your Judgment at once, and my Passion You wrong:
You take that for Fact, which will scarce be found Wit:
　　Od's Life! must One swear to the Truth of a Song?

What I speak, my fair CLOE, and what I write, shows
　　The Difference there is betwixt Nature and Art:
I court others in Verse; but I love Thee in Prose:
　　And They have my Whimsies; but Thou hast my
　　　　Heart.

The God of us Verse-men (You know Child) the SUN,
　　How after his Journeys He sets up his Rest:
If at Morning o'er Earth 'tis his Fancy to run;
　　At Night he reclines on his THETIS'S Breast.

So when I am wearied with wand'ring all Day;
　　To Thee my Delight in the Evening I come:
No Matter what Beauties I saw in my Way:
　　They were but my Visits; but Thou art my Home.

Then finish, Dear CLOE, this Pastoral War;
　　And let us like HORACE and LYDIA agree:
For Thou art a Girl as much brighter than Her.
　　As He was a Poet sublimer than Me.

A LETTER

TO THE HONOURABLE LADY MISS MARGARET-CAVENDISH-HOLLES-HARLEY

MY noble, lovely, little *Peggy*,
Let this my *First-Epistle*, beg ye,
At dawn of morn, and close of even,
To lift your heart and hands to heaven:

In double duty say your prayer,
Our father first, then *notre père;*
And, dearest *Child*, along the day,
In every thing you do and say,
Obey and please my *Lord* and *Lady*,
So *God* shall love, and *Angels* aid, ye.
  If to these *Precepts* You attend,
  No *Second-Letter* need I send,
  And so I rest Your constant Friend.

GEORGE GRANVILLE, EARL OF LANSDOWNE (1667-1735)

ADIEU L'AMOUR

HERE end my Chains, and Thraldom cease,
If not in Joy, I'll live at least in Peace:
Since for the Pleasures of an Hour,
We must endure an Age of Pain,
I'll be this abject thing no more,
Love, give me back my Heart again.

Despair tormented first my Breast,
Now Falsehood, a more cruel Guest:
O! for the Peace of Humankind,
Make women longer true, or sooner kind;
With Justice, or with Mercy reign,
O Love! or give me back my Heart again.

JONATHAN SWIFT (1667-1745)

IN SICKNESS

'TIS true—then why should I repine
To see my Life so fast decline?
But why obscurely here alone,
Where I am neither loved nor known?
My State of Health none care to learn;
My Life is here no Soul's Concern:
And those with whom I now converse
Without a Tear will tend my Hearse.

Removed from kind *Arbuthnot's* Aid,
Who knows his Art, but not the Trade,
Preferring his Regard for me
Before his Credit, or his Fee.
Some formal Visits, Looks, and Words,
What mere Humanity affords,
I meet perhaps from three or four,
From whom I once expected more;
Which those who tend the Sick for Pay,
Can act as decently as they:
But, no obliging, tender Friend,
To help at my approaching End.
My Life is now a Burden grown
To others, ere it be my own.
  Ye formal Weepers for the Sick,
In your last Offices be quick;
And spare my absent Friends the Grief
To hear, yet give me no Relief;
Expir'd To-day, entomb'd To-morrow,
When known, will save a double Sorrow.

DR. SWIFT TO MR. POPE

WHILE HE WAS WRITING THE DUNCIAD

Pope has the Talent well to speak,
  But not to reach the Ear;
His loudest Voice is low and weak,
  The Dean too deaf to hear.

A while they on each other look,
  Then different Studies choose;
The *Dean* sits plodding on a Book;
  Pope walks, and courts the Muse.

Now Backs of Letters, though design'd
  For those who more will need 'em,
Are fill'd with Hints, and interlin'd,
  Himself can hardly read 'em!

Each Atom by some other struck,
  All Turns and Motions tries;
Till in a Lump together stuck,
  Behold a *Poem* rise!

Yet to the *Dean* his share allot;
  He claims it by a Canon;
That, without which a Thing is not,
  Is *causa sine quâ non.*

Thus, *Pope*, in vain you boast your Wit;
  For, had our deaf Divine
Been for your Conversation fit,
  You had not writ a Line.

Of Prelate thus, for preaching fam'd
  The Sexton reason'd well;
And justly half the Merit claim'd,
  Because he *rang the Bell.*

ON THE DEATH OF DR. SWIFT

As *Rochfoucault* his Maxims drew
From Nature, I believe 'em true:
They argue no corrupted Mind
In him; the Fault is in Mankind.
  . . . .
Vain human Kind! Fantastic Race!
Thy various Follies who can trace?
Self-love, Ambition, Envy, Pride,
Their Empire in our Hearts divide.
Give others Riches, Power and Station,
'Tis all on me an Usurpation.
I have no Title to aspire;
Yet, when you sink, I seem the higher.
In *Pope* I cannot read a line,
But with a Sigh I wish it mine;
When He can in one Couplet fix
More Sense than I can do in six;

It gives me such a jealous Fit,
I cry " Pox take him and his Wit ! "
I grieve to be outdone by *Gay*
In my own hum'rous biting Way.
Arbuthnot is no more my Friend,
Who dares to Irony pretend,
Which I was born to introduce,
Refin'd it first and show'd its Use.
St. John, as well as *Pultney*, knows
That I had some Repute for Prose ;
And till they drove me out of Date
Could maul a Minister of State.
If they have mortify'd my Pride,
And made me throw my Pen aside ;
If with such Talents Heav'n has blest 'em,
Have I not Reason to detest 'em ?
 To all my Foes, dear Fortune, send
Thy Gifts ; but never to my Friend :
I tamely can endure the first ;
But this with Envy makes me burst.
Thus much may serve by way of Proem :
Proceed we therefore to our Poem.
 The Time is not remote, when I
Must by the Course of Nature die ;

 . . . . .

My good Companions, never fear ;
For though you may mistake a Year,
Though your Prognostics run too fast,
They must be verified at last.
 Behold the fatal Day arrive !
" How is the Dean ? "—" He's just alive."
Now the departing Prayer is read ;
" He hardly breathes "—" The Dean is dead."
 Before the Passing Bell begun,
The News through half the Town has run.
" O ! may we all for Death prepare !
What has he left ? and who's his Heir ? "—
" I know no more than what the News is ;
'Tis all bequeath'd to Public Uses."

"To Public Uses! there's a Whim!
What had the Public done for him?
Mere Envy, Avarice, and Pride:
He gave it all—but first he died.
And had the Dean, in all the Nation,
No worthy Friend, No poor Relation?
So ready to do Strangers good,
Forgetting his own Flesh and Blood!"
   Now, Grub Street Wits are all employ'd;
With Elegies the Town is cloy'd:
Some Paragraph in ev'ry Paper
To *curse* the *Dean*, or *bless* the *Drapier*.
   The Doctors, tender of their Fame,
Wisely on me lay all the Blame:
"We must confess, his Case was nice;
But he would never take Advice.
Had he been rul'd, for aught appears,
He might have liv'd these twenty Years;
For, when we open'd him, we found,
That all his vital Parts were sound."
   From *Dublin* soon to *London* spread,
'Tis told at court, "the Dean is dead."
Kind Lady *Suffolk* in the Spleen
Runs laughing up to tell the Queen.
The Queen so Gracious, Mild, and Good,
Cries, "Is he gone? 'Tis time he should.
He's dead you say; then let him rot;
I'm glad the Medals were forgot.
I promis'd him, I own; but when?
I only was the Princess then."

. . .

Now *Curll* his Shop from Rubbish drains:
Three genuine Tomes of *Swift's* remains!
And then to make them pass the glibber,
Revis'd by *Tibbalds*, *Moore* and *Cibber*.
He'll treat me as he does my Betters,
Publish my Will, my Life, my Letters:
Revive the Libels born to die;
Which *Pope* must bear, as well as I.

Here shift the Scene, to represent
How those I love my Death lament.
Poor *Pope* would grieve a month, and *Gay*
A week, and *Arbuthnot* a day.
St. *John* himself will scarce forbear
To bite his Pen, and drop a Tear.
The rest will give a Shrug, and Cry,
" I'm sorry but we all must die ! "

. . . .

My female Friends, whose tender Hearts
Have better learn'd to act their Parts,
Receive the News in doleful Dumps :
" The Dean is dead : (Pray what is Trumps ?)
Then, Lord, have Mercy on his Soul !
(Ladies, I'll venture for the Vole.)
Six Deans, they say, must bear the Pall :
(I wish I knew what King to call.)
Madam, your Husband will attend
The Funeral, of so good a Friend.
No, Madam, 'tis a shocking Sight :
And he's engag'd to-morrow Night :
My Lady Club would take it ill,
If he should fail her at Quadrille.
He lov'd the Dean—(I lead a Heart,)
But dearest Friends, they say, must part.
His Time was come : he ran his Race ;
We hope he's in a better Place."
Why do we grieve that Friends should die ?
No Loss more easy to supply.

One Year is past ; a different Scene !
No further mention of the Dean ;
Who now, alas ! no more is missed,
Than if he never did exist.
Where's now this favourite of *Apollo* ?
Departed :—*And his works must follow* :
Some Country Squire to *Lintot* goes,
Inquires for *Swift* in Verse and Prose.

Says *Lintot*, "I have heard the name;
He died a Year ago."—"The same."
He searches all the Shop in vain.
"Sir, you may find them in *Duck Lane*;
I sent them, with a Load of Books,
Last Monday to the Pastry Cook's.
To fancy, they could live a Year!
I find, you're but a Stranger here.
The Dean was famous in his Time,
And had a kind of Knack at Rhyme
His way of Writing now is past:
The Town has got a better Taste;
I keep no antiquated Stuff,
But Spick and Span I have enough.
Pray do but give me leave to show 'em;
Here's *Colley Cibber's* Birthday poem.
This Ode you never yet have seen,
By *Stephen Duck* upon the Queen.
Then, here's a Letter finely penn'd
Against the Craftsman and his Friend:
It clearly shows that all Reflection
On Ministers is Disaffection.

. . . . .

"Perhaps I may allow, the Dean,
Had too much Satire in his Vein;
And seem'd determin'd not to starve it,
Because no Age could more deserve it.
Yet Malice never was his Aim;
He lash'd the Vice, but spar'd the Name;
No Individual could resent,
Where Thousands equally were meant;
His satire points at no Defect,
But what all Mortals may correct;
For he abhorr'd that senseless Tribe
Who call it Humour when they jibe:
He spar'd a Hump, or crooked Nose,
Whose Owners set not up for Beaux.
True genuine Dullness mov'd his Pity,
Unless it offer'd to be witty.

Those who their Ignorance confess'd,
He ne'er offended with a Jest;
But laugh'd to hear an Idiot quote
A verse from *Horace* learn'd by Rote.
Vice if it e'er can be abash'd,
Must be or *Ridicul'd* or *Lash'd*.
If you *resent* it, who's to blame?
He neither knew *you* nor your *Name*.
Should Vice expect to 'scape Rebuke,
Because its Owner is a Duke?
 "He knew a hundred pleasant Stories,
With all the Turns of *Whigs* and *Tories*:
Was cheerful to his dying Day;
His Friends would let him have his Way.
 "He gave the little Wealth he had
To build a House for Fools and Mad;
And shew'd by one satiric Touch,
No Nation wanted it so much.
That Kingdom he had left his Debtor,
I wish it soon may have a better.
And, since you dread no farther Lashes
Methinks you may forgive his Ashes."

WILLIAM CONGREVE (1670–1729)

FALSE though she be to me and Love,
 I'll ne'er pursue Revenge;
For still the Charmer I approve,
 Though I deplore her Change.

In Hours of Bliss we oft have met,
 They could not always last;
And though the present I regret,
 I'm grateful for the past.

JOSEPH ADDISON (1672–1719)

THE Spacious Firmament on high,
With all the blue Ethereal Sky,
And spangled Heav'ns, a Shining Frame,
Their great Original proclaim;

Th' unwearied Sun, from day to day,
Doth his Creator's Power display,
And publishes to every Land
The Work of an Almighty Hand.

Soon as the Ev'ning Shades prevail,
The Moon takes up the wondrous Tale,
And nightly to the list'ning Earth
Repeats the Story of her Birth:
Whilst all the Stars that round her burn,
And all the Planets in their turn,
Confirm the Tidings as they roll
And spread the Truth from Pole to Pole.

What tho', in solemn Silence, all
Move round the dark terrestrial Ball?
What tho' nor real Voice nor Sound
Amid their radiant Orbs be found?
In Reason's Ear they all rejoice,
And utter forth a glorious Voice,
For ever singing as they shine,
" The Hand that made us is Divine."

ISAAC WATTS (1674–1748)

SIGHT THROUGH A GLASS, AND FACE TO FACE

I LOVE the Windows of thy Grace
  Through which my Lord is seen,
And long to meet my Saviour's Face
  Without a Glass between.

O that the happy Hour were come,
  To change my Faith to Sight!
I shall behold my Lord at Home
  In a diviner Light.

Haste, my Beloved, and remove
  These interposing Days;
Then shall my Passions all be Love,
  And all my Pow'rs be Praise.

THE CHURCH THE GARDEN OF CHRIST

We are a Garden wall'd around,
Chosen and made peculiar Ground;
A little Spot inclos'd by Grace,
Out of the World's wide Wilderness.

Like Trees of Myrrh and Spice we stand
Planted by God the Father's Hand;
And all his Springs in *Sion* flow,
To make the young Plantation grow.

Awake, O heavenly Wind, and come,
Blow on this Garden of perfume;
Spirit Divine, descend and breathe
A gracious Gale on Plants beneath.

Make our best Spices flow abroad,
To entertain our Saviour God:
And Faith and Love and Joy appear,
And every Grace be active here.

Let my beloved come, and taste
His pleasant Fruits at his own Feast.
I come, my Spouse, I come, he cries,
With Love and Pleasure in his Eyes.

Our Lord into his Garden comes,
Well pleas'd to smell our poor Perfumes,
And calls us to a Feast divine,
Sweeter than Honey, Milk, or Wine.

Eat of the Tree of Life, my Friends,
The Blessings that my Father sends;
Your Taste shall all my Dainties prove,
And drink abundance of my Love.

Jesus, we will frequent Thy Board,
And sing the Bounties of our Lord:
And the rich Food on which we live
Demands more Praise than Tongues can give.

MAN FRAIL AND GOD ETERNAL

Our God, our Help in Ages past,
  Our Hope for Years to come,
Our Shelter from the stormy Blast,
  And our eternal Home.

Under the Shadow of Thy Throne
  Thy Saints have dwelt secure;
Sufficient is thine Arm alone,
  And our Defence is sure.

Before the Hills in order stood
  Or Earth receiv'd her Frame,
From everlasting Thou art God,
  To endless Years the same.

Thy Word commands our Flesh to Dust,
  Return, ye Sons of Men.
All Nations rose from Earth at first,
  And turn to Earth again.

A thousand Ages in thy Sight
  Are like an Evening gone;
Short as the Watch that ends the Night
  Before the rising Sun.

The busy Tribes of Flesh and Blood
  With all their Lives and Cares
Are carried downwards by thy Flood,
  And lost in following Years.

Time like an ever-rolling Stream
  Bears all its Sons away;
They fly forgotten as a Dream
  Dies at the opening Day.

Like flow'ry Fields the Nations stand
  Pleas'd with the Morning-light;
The Flowers beneath the Mower's Hand
  Lie withering e'er 'tis Night.

Our God, our Help in Ages past,
Our Hope for Years to come,
Be Thou our Guard while Troubles last
And our eternal Home.

AMBROSE PHILIPS (1675-1749)
SONG

FROM *White's* and *Will's*
To purling Rills
The Love-sick *Strephon* flies;
There, full of Woe,
His Numbers flow,
And all in Rhyme he dies.

The fair Coquet,
With feign'd Regret,
Invites him back to Town;
But when, in Tears,
The Youth appears,
She meets him with a Frown.

Full oft' the Maid
This Prank had play'd,
'Till angry *Strephon* swore;
And, what is strange,
Tho' loth to change,
Would never see her more.

JOHN GAY (1685-1732).

From THE SHEPHERD'S WEEK
TUESDAY; OR, THE DITTY
Marian

YOUNG *Colin Clout*, a Lad of peerless *Meed*,
Full well could dance, and deftly tune the Reed;
In every Wood his Carols sweet were known,
In ev'ry Wake his nimble Feats were shown.

When in the Ring the Rustic Routs he threw,
The Damsels' Pleasures with his Conquests grew;
Or when aslant the Cudgel threats his Head,
His Danger smites the Breast of ev'ry Maid,
But chief of *Marian*. *Marian* lov'd the Swain,
The Parson's Maid, and neatest of the Plain.
Marian, that soft could strok the udder'd Cow,
Or with her Winnow ease the Barly-Mow;
Marbled with Sage the hard'ning Cheese she press'd
And yellow Butter *Marian's* Skill confess'd;
But *Marian* now devoid of Country Cares,
Nor yellow Butter, nor Sage Cheese prepares.
For yearning Love the witless Maid employs,
And *Love* say Swains, *all busie Heed destroys*.
Colin makes mock at all her piteous Smart,
A lass that *Cic'ly* hight, had won his Heart,
Cic'ly the Western Lass, that tends the *Kee*,[1]
The Rival of the Parson's Maid was she.
In dreary Shade now *Marian* lies along,
And mixt with Sighs thus wails in plaining Song.

   Ah woful Day! ah woful Noon and Morn!
When first by thee my Younglings white were shorn;
Then first, I ween, I cast a Lover's Eye,
My Sheep were silly, but more silly I.
Beneath the Shears they felt no lasting Smart,
They lost but Fleeces while I lost a Heart.

   Ah, *Colin*! canst thou leave thy Sweetheart true!
What I have done for thee, will *Cic'ly* do?
Will she thy Linen wash or Hosen darn,
And knit thee Gloves made of her own-spun Yarn?
Will she with Huswife's Hand provide thy Meat,
And ev'ry *Sunday* Morn thy Neckcloth plait?
Which o'er thy Kersey Doublet spreading wide,
In Service-Time drew *Cic'ly's* Eyes aside.

   Where'er I gad I cannot hide my Care,
My new Disasters in my Look appear.
White as the Curd my ruddy Cheek is grown,
So thin my Features, that I'm hardly known;

   [1] Kee, *a West-Country Word for* Kine *or* Cows.

Our Neighbours tell me oft, in joking Talk,
Of Ashes, Leather, Oatmeal, Bran, and Chalk;
Unwittingly of *Marian* they divine;
And wist not that with thoughtful Love I pine.
Yet *Colin Clout*, untoward Shepherd Swain,
Walks whistling blithe, while pitiful I plain.
   Whilom with thee 'twas *Marian's* dear Delight
To moil all Day, and merry-make at Night.
If in the Soil you guide the crooked Share,
Your early Breakfast is my constant Care.
And when with even Hand you strow the Grain,
I fright the thievish Rooks from off the Plain.
In misling Days when I my Thresher heard,
With nappy Beer I to the Barn repair'd;
Lost in the Music of the whirling Flail,
To gaze on thee I left the Smoking Pail:
In Harvest when the sun was mounted high,
My Leathern Bottle did thy Drought supply;
Whene'er you mow'd, I follow'd with the Rake,
And have full oft been Sun-burnt for thy Sake;
When in the Welkin gath'ring Show'rs were seen,
I lagg'd the last with *Colin* on the Green;
And when at Eve returning with thy Car,
Awaiting heard the gingling Bells from far,
Straight on the Fire the sooty Pot I plac't,
To warm thy Broth I burnt my Hands for Haste.
When hungry thou stood'st *staring like an Oaf*,
I slic'd the Luncheon from the Barly-Loaf;
With crumbled Bread I thicken'd well thy Mess.
Ah, love me more, or love thy Pottage less!
   Last *Friday's* Eve, when as the Sun was set,
I, near yon Stile, three sallow Gypsies met.
Upon my Hand they cast a poring Look,
Bid me beware, and thrice their Heads they shook,
They said that many Crosses I must prove,
Some in my worldly Gain, but most in Love.
Next Morn I miss'd three Hens and our old Cock,
And off the Hedge two Pinners and a Smock.

I bore these Losses with a Christian Mind,
And no Mishaps could feel, while thou wert kind.
But since, alas! I grew my *Colin's* Scorn,
I've known no Pleasure, Night or Noon, or Morn.
Help me, ye Gypsies, bring him home again,
And to a constant Lass give back her Swain.
  Have I not sat with thee full many a Night,
When dying Embers were our only Light,
When ev'ry Creature did in Slumbers lie,
Besides our Cat, my *Colin Clout*, and I?
No troublous Thoughts the Cat or *Colin* move,
While I alone am kept awake by Love.
  Remember, *Colin*, when at last Year's Wake,
I bought the costly Present for thy Sake,
Could'st thou spell o'er the Posy on thy Knife,
And with another change thy State of Life?
If thou forgett'st, I wot, I can repeat,
My Memory can tell the Verse so sweet.
As this is grav'd upon this Knife of thine,
So is thy Image on this Heart of mine.
But Woe is me! Such Presents luckless prove,
For Knives, they tell me, *always sever Love*,
  Thus Marian wail'd, her Eyes with Tears brimful,
When Goody *Dobbins* brought her Cow to Bull.
With Apron blue to dry her Tears she sought,
Then saw the Cow well serv'd, and took a Groat.

THURSDAY; OR, THE SPELL

Hobnelia

Hobnelia seated in a dreary Vale,
In pensive Mood rehears'd her piteous Tale,
Her piteous Tale the Winds in Sighs bemoan,
And pining Echo answers Groan for Groan.

  "I rue the Day, a rueful Day I trow,
The woful Day, a Day indeed of Woe!
When *Lubberkin* to Town his Cattle drove,
A Maiden fine bedight he hapt to love;

The Maiden fine bedight his Love retains,
And for the Village he forsakes the Plains :
Return, my *Lubberkin*, these Ditties hear ;
Spells will I try, and Spells shall ease my Care.
    *With my sharp Heel I three times mark the Ground,
And turn me thrice around, around, around.*

    " When first the Year, I heard the Cuckoo sing,
And call with welcome Note the budding Spring,
I straightway set a running with such Haste,
Deb'rah, that won the Smock, scarce ran so fast.
'Till spent for lack of Breath, quite weary grown,
Upon a rising Bank I sat adown,
Then doff'd my Shoe, and by my Troth, I swear,
Therein I spy'd this yellow frizzled Hair,
As like to *Lubberkin's* in Curl and Hue,
As if upon his comely Pate it grew.
    *With my sharp Heel I three times mark the Ground,
And turn me thrice around, around, around.*

    " At Eve last *Midsummer* no Sleep I sought,
But to the Field a Bag of Hemp-seed brought,
I scatter'd round the Seed on ev'ry side,
And three times in a trembling Accent cry'd,
*This Hemp-seed with my Virgin Hand I sow,
Who shall my True-love be, the Crop shall mow.*
I straight look'd back, and if my Eyes speak Truth,
With his keen Scythe behind me came the Youth.
    *With my sharp Heel I three times mark the Ground,
And turn me thrice around, around, around.*

    " Last *Valentine*, the Day when Birds of Kind
Their Paramours with mutual Chirpings find ;
I rearly rose, just at the break of Day,
Before the sun had chas'd the Stars away ;
Afield I went, amid the Morning Dew
To milk my Kine (for so should Huswives do)
Thee first I spy'd ; and the first Swain we see,
In spite of Fortune, shall our True-love be ;

See, *Lubberkin*, each Bird his Partner take,
And can'st thou then thy Sweetheart dear forsake?
*With my sharp Heel I three times mark the Ground,
And turn me thrice around, around, around.*

" Last *May-day* fair I search'd to find a Snail
That might my secret Lover's Name reveal;
Upon a Gooseberry-Bush a Snail I found,
For always Snails near sweetest Fruit abound.
I seiz'd the Vermin, home I quickly sped,
And on the Hearth the milk-white Embers spread.
Slow crawl'd the Snail, and if I right can spell,
In the soft Ashes mark'd a curious *L*:
Oh, may this wondrous Omen lucky prove!
For *L* is found in *Lubberkin* and *Love*.
*With my sharp Heel I three times mark the Ground,
And turn me thrice around, around, around.*

" Two Hazel Nuts I threw into the Flame,
And to each Nut I gave a Sweet-heart's Name.
This with the loudest Bounce me sore amaz'd,
That in a Flame of brightest Colour blaz'd.
As blaz'd the Nut, so may thy Passion grow,
For 'twas *thy Nut* that did so brightly glow.
*With my sharp Heel I three times mark the Ground,
And turn me thrice around, around, around.*

" As Peascods once I pluck'd, I chanc'd to see
One that was closely fill'd with three times three,
Which when I cropped, I safely home convey'd,
And o'er the Door the Spell in secret laid.
My Wheel I turn'd, and sung a Ballad new,
While from the Spindle I the Fleeces drew;
The Latch mov'd up, when who should first come in,
But in his proper person—*Lubberkin*.
I broke my Yarn surprised the Sight to see,
Sure Sign that he would break his Word with me.
Eftsoons I join'd it with my wonted Slight:
So may again his Love with mine unite!
*With my sharp Heel I three times mark the Ground,
And turn me thrice around, around, around.*

"This *Lady-fly* I take from off the Grass,
Whose spotted Back might scarlet Red surpass.
Fly, lady-bird, North, South, or East, or West,
Fly where the Man is found that I love best.
He leaves my Hand, see to the *West* he's flown,
To call my True-love from the faithless Town,
   With my sharp Heel I three times mark the Ground,
And turn me thrice around, around, around.

"This mellow Pippin which I pare around
My Shepherd's Name shall flourish on the Ground.
I fling th' unbroken Paring o'er my head,
Upon the Grass a perfect *L* is read;
Yet on my Heart a fairer *L* is seen
Than what the Paring marks upon the Green.
   With my sharp Heel I three times mark the Ground,
And turn me thrice around, around, around. . . .

"As I was wont, I trudg'd last Market-Day
To Town, with New-laid Eggs preserv'd in Hay.
I made my Market long before 'twas Night,
My Purse grew heavy and my Basket light.
Straight to the Pothecary's Shop I went,
And in Love-Powder all my Money spent;
Behap what will, next Sunday, after Prayers,
When to the Ale-house *Lubberkin* repairs,
These Golden Flies into his Mug I'll throw,
And soon the Swain with fervent Love shall glow.
   With my sharp Heel I three times mark the Ground,
And turn me thrice around, around, around.

"But hold—our *Lightfoot* barks, and cocks his Ears,
O'er yonder Stile see *Lubberkin* appears.
He comes, he comes, *Hobnelia's* not bewrayed,
Nor shall she crown'd with Willow die a Maid.
He vows, he swears, he'll give me a green Gown,
Oh dear! I fall *adown, adown, adown!*"

EPISTLE

TO THE RIGHT HONOURABLE
PAUL METHUEN, Esq.

Yes, I'll maintain what you have often said,
That 'tis encouragement makes Science spread ;
True generous Spirits prosperous vice detest,
And love to cherish virtue when distressed :
But e'er our mighty Lords this scheme pursue,
Our mighty Lords must think and act like you.
    Why must we climb the *Alpine* mountain's sides
To find the seat where Harmony resides ?
Why touch we not so soft the silver lute,
The cheerful haut-boy, and the mellow flute ?
'Tis not th' *Italian* clime improves the sound,
But there the Patrons of her sons are found.

    Why flourish'd verse in great *Augustus'* reign ?
He and Mecænas lov'd the Muse's strain.
But now that wight in poverty must mourn
Who was (O cruel stars !) a Poet born.
Yet there are ways for authors to be great ;
Write ranc'rous libels to reform the State ;
Of if you choose more sure and readier ways,
Spatter a Minister with fulsome praise :
Launch out with freedom, flatter him enough ;
Fear not, all men are dedication-proof,
Be bolder yet, you must go farther still,
Dip deep in gall thy mercenary quill.
He, who his pen in party quarrels draws,
Lists a hir'd bravo to support the cause ;
He must indulge his Patron's hate and spleen,
And stab the fame of those he ne'er has seen.
Why then should authors mourn their desperate case ?
Be brave, do this, and then demand a place.
Why art thou poor ? exert the gifts to rise,
And banish tim'rous virtue from thy eyes.

All this seems modern preface, where we're told
That wit is prais'd, but hungry lives and cold:
Against th' ungrateful age these authors roar,
And fancy learning starves because they're poor.
Yet why should learning hope success at Court?
Why should our Patriots virtue's cause support?
Why to true merit should they have regard?
They know that virtue is its own reward.
Yet let not me of grievances complain,
Who (though the meanest of the Muse's train)
Can boast subscriptions to my humble lays,
And mingle profit with my little praise.

    Ask Painting, why she loves *Hesperian* air.
Go view, she cries, my glorious labours there:
There in rich palaces I reign in state,
And on the temple's lofty domes create.
The Nobles view my works with knowing eyes,
They love the science, and the painter prize.

    Had *Pope* with grovelling numbers fill'd his page,
Dennis had never kindled into rage.
'Tis the sublime that hurts the Critic's ease;
Write nonsense, and he reads and sleeps in peace.
Were *Prior*, *Congreve*, *Swift* and *Pope* unknown,
Poor slander-selling *Curll* would be undone.
He who would free from malice pass his days,
Must live obscure, and never merit praise.
But let this tale to valiant virtue tell
The daily perils of deserving well.

    A crow was strutting o'er the stubbled plain,
Just as a lark descending clos'd his strain.
The crow bespoke him thus with solemn grace.
Thou most accomplish'd of the feather'd race,
What force of lungs! how clear! how sweet you sing!
And no bird soars upon a stronger wing.
The lark, who scorn'd soft flatt'ry, thus replies,
True, I sing sweet, and on strong pinion rise;

Yet let me pass my life from envy free,
For what advantage are these gifts to me?
My song confines me to the wiry cage,
My flight provokes the falcon's fatal rage.
But as you pass, I hear the fowlers say,
To shoot at crows is powder flung away.

AN ELEGY ON A LAP-DOG

Shock's fate I mourn; poor *Shock* is now no more,
Ye Muses mourn, ye chamber-maids deplore.
Unhappy *Shock*! yet more unhappy Fair,
Doom'd to survive thy joy and only care!
Thy wretched fingers now no more shall deck,
And tie the favourite ribbon round his neck;
No more thy hand shall smooth his glossy hair,
And comb the wavings of his pendent ear.
Yet cease thy flowing grief, forsaken maid;
All mortal pleasures in a moment fade:
Our surest hope is in an hour destroy'd,
And love, best gift of heav'n, not long enjoy'd.

Methinks I see her frantic with despair,
Her streaming eyes, wrung hands, and flowing hair;
Her *Mechlen* pinners rent the floor bestrow,
And her torn fan gives real signs of woe.
Hence Superstition, that tormenting guest,
That haunts with fancy'd fears the coward breast;
No dread events upon this fate attend,
Stream eyes no more, no more thy tresses rend.
Tho' certain omens oft forewarn a state,
And dying lions show the monarch's fate;
Why should such fears bid *Celia's* sorrow rise?
For when a Lap-dog falls, no lover dies.

Cease, *Celia*, cease; restrain thy flowing tears,
Some warmer passion will dispel thy cares.
In man you'll find a more substantial bliss,
More grateful toying, and a sweeter kiss.

He's dead. Oh lay him gently in the ground!
And may his tomb be by this verse renown'd.
Here Shock, *the pride of all his kind, is laid;*
Who fawn'd like man, but ne'er like man betray'd.

THE LADY'S LAMENTATION

PHYLLIDA, that lov'd to dream
In the grove, or by the stream;
   Sigh'd on velvet pillow.
What, alas! should fill her head,
But a fountain, or a mead,
   Water and a willow?

"Love in cities never dwells,
He delights in rural cells
   Which sweet woodbine covers.
What are your *Assemblys* then?
There, 'tis true, we see more men;
   But much fewer lovers.

"Oh, how chang'd the prospect grows!
Flocks and herds to Fops and Beaus,
   Coxcombs without number!
Moon and stars that shone so bright,
To the torch and waxen light,
   And whole nights at *Ombre*.

"Pleasant as it is, to hear
Scandal tickling in our ear,
   Ev'n of our own mothers;
In the chit-chat of the day,
To us is pay'd, when we're away,
   What we lent to others.

"Though the fav'rite *Toast* I reign;
Wine, they say, that prompts the vain,
   Heightens defamation.
Must I live 'twixt spite and fear,
Ev'ry day grow handsomer,
   And lose my reputation?"

Thus the Fair to sighs gave way,
Her empty purse beside her lay.
　Nymph, ah cease thy sorrow.
Though curst fortune frown to-night;
This odious town can give delight,
　If you win to-morrow.

SWEET WILLIAM'S FAREWELL TO BLACK-EY'D SUSAN

ALL in the *Downs* the fleet was moor'd,
　The streamers waving in the wind,
When black-ey'd *Susan* came aboard.
" Oh! where shall I my true-love find!
Tell me, ye jovial sailors, tell me true,
If my sweet *William* sails among the crew."

William, who high upon the yard
　Rock'd with the billow to and fro,
Soon as her well-known voice he heard,
He sigh'd, and cast his eyes below:
The cord slides swiftly through his glowing hands,
And (quick as lightning) on the deck he stands.

So the sweet lark, high-pois'd in air,
　Shuts close his pinions to his breast,
(If, chance, his mate's shrill call he hear)
　And drops at once into her nest.
The noblest Captain in the *British* fleet
Might envy *William's* lips those kisses sweet.

" O *Susan, Susan*, lovely dear,
　My vows shall ever true remain;
Let me kiss off that falling tear,
　We only part to meet again.
Change, as ye list, ye winds; my heart shall be
The faithful compass that still points to thee.

" Believe not what the landmen say,
    Who tempt with doubts thy constant mind :
They'll tell thee, sailors, when away,
    In every port a mistress find.
Yes, yes, believe them when they tell thee so,
For thou art present whereso'er I go.

" If to far *India's* coast we sail,
    Thy eyes are seen in diamonds bright,
Thy breath is *Africk's* spicy gale,
    Thy skin is ivory, so white.
Thus every beauteous object that I view,
Wakes in my soul some charm of lovely *Sue*.

" Though battle call me from thy arms,
    Let not my pretty *Susan* mourn ;
Though cannons roar, yet safe from har.ns,
    William shall to his Dear return.
Love turns aside the balls that round me fly,
Lest precious tears should drop from *Susan's* eye."

The boatswain gave the dreadful word,
    The sails their swelling bosom spread,
No longer must she stay aboard :
    They kiss'd, she sigh'd, he hung his head.
Her less'ning boat, unwilling rows to land :
" Adieu " she cries ! and wav'd her lily hand.

FABLE XXXVII

The FARMER'S WIFE *and the* RAVEN

WHY are those tears ? Why droops your head ?
Is then your other husband dead ?
Or does a worse disgrace betide ?
Hath no one since his death apply'd ?
    Alas ! you know the cause too well,
The salt is spilt, to me it fell.
Then, to contribute to my loss,
My knife and fork were laid across,

On *friday* too ! the day I dread !
Would I were safe at home in bed !
Last night (I vow to Heav'n 'tis true)
Bounce from the fire a coffin flew.
Next post some fatal news shall tell.
God send my *Cornish* friends be well !
   Unhappy widow, cease thy tears,
Nor feel affliction in thy fears,
Let not thy stomach be suspended,
Eat now, and weep when dinner's ended,
And when the butler clears the table
For thy dessert I'll read my fable.
   Betwixt her swagging pannier's load
A Farmer's wife to market rode,
And, jogging on, with thoughtful care
Summ'd up the profits of her ware ;
When, starting from her silver dream,
Thus far and wide was heard her scream :
   That raven on yon left-hand oak
(Curse on his ill-betiding croak)
Bodes me no good. No more she said,
When poor blind *Ball* with stumbling tread
Fell prone ; o'erturned the pannier lay,
And her mash'd eggs bestrow'd the way.
   She, sprawling in the yellow road,
Rail'd, swore and curst. Thou croaking toad.
A murrain take thy whoreson throat !
I knew misfortune in the note.
   Dame, quoth the Raven, spare your oaths,
Unclench your fist, and wipe your clothes.
But why on me those curses thrown ?
Goody, the fault was all your own ;
For had you laid this brittle ware
On *Dun*, the old sure-footed mare,
Though all the Ravens of the *Hundred*
With croaking had your tongue out-thunder'd,
Sure-footed *Dun* had kept her legs,
And you, good woman, sav'd your eggs

SONG

Youth's the Season made for Joys,
   Love is then our Duty,
She alone who that employs,
   Well deserves her Beauty.
      Let's be gay,
      While we may,
Beauty's a Flower, despis'd in decay.

Let us drink and sport to-day,
   Ours is not to-morrow.
Love with Youth flies swift away,
   Age is nought but Sorrow.
      Dance and sing,
      Time's on the Wing,
Life never knows the return of Spring.

SONG

O RUDDIER than the Cherry,
O sweeter than the Berry,
   O Nymph more bright
   Than Moonshine Night
Like Kidlings blithe and merry.
Ripe as the Melting Cluster
No Lily has such Lustre,
   Yet hard to tame
   As raging Flame
And fierce as Storms that bluster.

ANONYMOUS (1726)

EPITAPH ON TOM D'URFEY

HERE lies the *Lyrick*, who with Tale and Song,
Did Life to threescore Years and ten prolong:
His Tale was pleasant, and his Song was sweet;
His Heart was cheerful—but his Thirst was great.
Grieve, Reader, grieve, that he, too soon grown old,
His Song has ended, and his Tale has told.

ALEXANDER POPE (1688-1744)
THE RAPE OF THE LOCK
From Canto I

WHAT dire offence from am'rous causes springs,
What mighty contests rise from trivial things,
I sing—This verse to CARYL, Muse! is due:
This, ev'n Belinda may vouchsafe to view:
Slight is the subject, but not so the praise,
If She inspire, and He approve my lays.
   Say what strange motive, Goddess! could compel
A well-bred Lord t' assault a gentle Belle?
O say what stranger cause, yet unexplor'd,
Could make a gentle Belle reject a Lord?
In tasks so bold, can little men engage,
And in soft bosoms dwells such mighty Rage?
   Sol thro' white curtains shot a tim'rous ray,
And oped those eyes that must eclipse the day:
Now lap-dogs give themselves the rousing shake,
And sleepless lovers, just at twelve, awake:
Thrice rung the bell, the slipper knock'd the ground,
And the press'd watch return'd a silver sound.
Belinda still her downy pillow prest,
Her guardian SYLPH prolong'd the balmy rest:
'Twas He had summon'd to her silent bed
The morning-dream that hover'd o'er her head;
A Youth more glitt'ring than a Birth-night Beau,
(That ev'n in slumber caus'd her cheek to glow)
Seem'd to her ear his winning lips to lay,
And thus in whispers said, or seem'd to say.
   Fairest of mortals, thou distinguish'd care
Of thousand bright Inhabitants of Air!
If e'er one vision touch'd thy infant thought,
Of all the Nurse and all the Priest have taught;
Of airy Elves by moonlight shadows seen,
The silver token, and the circled green,
Or virgins visited by Angel-pow'rs,
With golden crowns and wreaths of heav'nly flow'rs;

Hear and believe ! thy own importance know,
Nor bound thy narrow views to things below.
Some secret truths, from learned pride conceal'd,
To Maids alone and Children are reveal'd :
What tho' no credit doubting Wits may give ?
The Fair and Innocent shall still believe.
Know, then, unnumber'd Spirits round thee fly,
The light Militia of the lower sky:
These, tho' unseen, are ever on the wing,
Hang o'er the Box, and hover round the Ring.
Think what an equipage thou hast in Air,
And view with scorn two Pages and a Chair.
As now your own, our beings were of old,
And once inclos'd in Woman's beauteous mould ;
Thence, by a soft transition, we repair
From earthly Vehicles to these of air,
Think not, when Woman's transient breath is fled,
That all her vanities at once are dead ;
Succeeding vanities she still regards,
And tho' she plays no more, o'erlooks the cards.
Her joy in gilded Chariots, when alive,
And love of Ombre, after death survive
For when the Fair in all their pride expire,
To their First Elements their Souls retire :
The Sprites of fiery Termagants in Flame
Mount up, and take a Salamander's name.
Soft yielding minds to Water glide away,
And sip, with Nymphs, their elemental Tea.
The graver Prude sinks downward to a Gnome,
In search of mischief still on Earth to roam.
The light Coquettes in Sylphs aloft repair,
And sport and flutter in the fields of Air. . . .
  Of these am I, who thy protection claim,
A watchful sprite, and Ariel is my name.
Late, as I rang'd the crystal wilds of air,
In the clear Mirror of thy ruling Star
I saw, alas ! some dread event impend,
Ere to the main this morning sun descend,

But heav'n reveals not what, or how, or where:
Warn'd by the Sylph, oh pious maid, beware!
This to disclose is all thy guardian can:
Beware of all, but most beware of Man!
   He said; when Shock, who thought she slept too long,
Leap'd up, and wak'd his mistress with his tongue.
'Twas then, Belinda, if report say true,
Thy eyes first open'd on a Billet-doux;
Wounds, Charms, and Ardors were no sooner read,
But all the Vision vanish'd from thy head.
   And now, unveil'd, the Toilet stands display'd,
Each silver Vase in mystic order laid.
First, rob'd in white, the Nymph intent adores,
With head uncover'd, the Cosmetic pow'rs.
A heav'nly image in the glass appears,
To that she bends, to that her eyes she rears;
Th' inferior Priestess, at her altar's side,
Trembling begins the sacred rites of Pride.
Unnumber'd treasures ope at once, and here
The various off'rings of the world appear;
From each she nicely culls with curious toil,
And decks the Goddess with the glitt'ring spoil.
This casket India's glowing gems unlocks,
And all Arabia breathes from yonder box.
The Tortoise here and Elephant unite,
Transform'd to combs, the speckled, and the white.
Here files of pins extend their shining rows,
Puffs, Powders, Patches, Bibles, Billet-doux.
Now awful Beauty puts on all its arms;
The fair each moment rises in her charms,
Repairs her smiles, awakens ev'ry grace,
And calls forth all the wonders of her face;
Sees by degrees a purer blush arise,
And keener lightnings quicken in her eyes.
The busy Sylphs surround their darling care,
These set the head, and those divide the hair,
Some fold the sleeve, whilst others plait the gown;
And Betty's prais'd for labours not her own.

ALEXANDER POPE

From CANTO II

NOT with more glories, in th' etherial plain,
The Sun first rises o'er the purpled main,
Than, issuing forth, the rival of his beams
Launch'd on the bosom of the silver Thames.
Fair Nymphs, and well-drest Youths around her shone,
But ev'ry eye was fix'd on her alone.
On her white breast a sparkling Cross she wore,
Which Jews might kiss, and Infidels adore.
Her lively looks a sprightly mind disclose,
Quick as her eyes, and as unfix'd as those:
Favours to none, to all she smiles extends;
Oft she rejects, but never once offends.
Bright as the sun, her eyes the gazers strike,
And, like the sun, they shine on all alike.
Yet graceful ease, and sweetness void of pride,
Might hide her faults, if Belles had faults to hide:
If to her share some female errors fall,
Look on her face, and you'll forget 'em all.
 This Nymph, to the destruction of mankind,
Nourish'd two Locks, which graceful hung behind
In equal curls, and well conspir'd to deck
With shining ringlets the smooth iv'ry neck.
Love in these labyrinths his slaves detains,
And mighty hearts are held in slender chains.
With hairy springes we the birds betray,
Slight lines of hair surprise the finny prey,
Fair tresses man's imperial race ensnare,
And beauty draws us with a single hair.
 Th' advent'rous Baron the bright locks admir'd;
He saw, he wish'd, and to the prize aspir'd.
Resolv'd to win, he meditates the way,
By force to ravish, or by fraud betray;
For when success a Lover's toil attends,
Few ask, if fraud or force attain'd his ends.
 For this, ere Phœbus rose, he had implor'd
Propitious heav'n, and ev'ry pow'r ador'd,
But chiefly Love—to Love an Altar built,
Of twelve vast French Romances, neatly gilt.

There lay three garters, half a pair of gloves;
And all the trophies of his former loves;
With tender Billet-doux he lights the pyre,
And breathes three am'rous sighs to raise the fire.
Then prostrate falls, and begs with ardent eyes
Soon to obtain, and long possess the prize:
The pow'rs gave ear, and granted half his pray'r,
The rest, the winds dispers'd in empty air. . . .

[ARIEL *speaks*]
  Ye Sylphs and Sylphids, to your chief give ear!
Fays, Fairies, Genii, Elves, and Dæmons, hear!
Ye know the spheres and various tasks assign'd
By laws eternal to th' aërial kind.
Some in the fields of purest Æther play,
And bask and whiten in the blaze of day.
Some guide the course of wand'ring orbs on high,
Or roll the planets thro' the boundless sky.
Some less refin'd, beneath the moon's pale light
Pursue the stars that shoot athwart the night,
Or suck the mists in grosser air below,
Or dip their pinions in the painted bow,
Or brew fierce tempests on the wintry main,
Or o'er the glebe distil the kindly rain.
Others on earth o'er human race preside,
Watch all their ways, and all their actions guide:
Of these the chief the care of Nations own,
And guard with Arms divine the British Throne.
  Our humbler province is to tend the Fair,
Not a less pleasing, tho' less glorious care;
To save the powder from too rude a gale,
Nor let th' imprison'd essences exhale;
To draw fresh colours from the vernal flow'rs;
To steal from rainbows e'er they drop in show'rs
A brighter wash; to curl their waving hairs,
Assist their blushes, and inspire their airs;
Nay oft, in dreams, invention we bestow,
To change a Flounce, or add a Furbelow.

This day, black Omens threat the brightest Fair,
That e'er deserv'd a watchful spirit's care ;
Some dire disaster, or by force or slight ;
But what, or where, the fates have wrapt in night.
Whether the nymph shall break Diana's law,
Or some frail China jar receive a flaw ;
Or stain her honour or her new brocade ;
Forget her pray'rs, or miss a masquerade ;
Or lose her heart, or necklace, at a ball ;
Or whether Heav'n has doom'd that Shock must fall.
Haste, then, ye spirits ! to your charge repair :
The flutt'ring fan be Zephyretta's care ;
The drops to thee, Brillante, we consign ;
And, Momentilla, let the watch be thine ;
Do thou, Crispissa, tend her fav'rite Lock ;
Ariel himself shall be the guard of Shock.
    To fifty chosen Sylphs, of special note,
We trust th' important charge, the Petticoat :
Oft have we known that seven-fold fence to fail,
Tho' stiff with hoops, and arm'd with ribs of whale ;
Form a strong line about the silver bound,
And guard the wide circumference around.
    Whatever spirit, careless of his charge,
His post neglects, or leaves the fair at large,
Shall feel sharp vengeance soon o'ertake his sins,
Be stopp'd in vials, or transfixed with pins ;
Or plung'd in lakes of bitter washes lie,
Or wedg'd whole ages in a bodkin's eye :
Gums and Pomatums shall his flight restrain,
While clogg'd he beats his silken wings in vain ;
Or Alum styptics with contracting pow'r
Shrink his thin essence like a rivel'd flow'r :
Or, as Ixion fix'd, the wretch shall feel
The giddy motion of the whirling Mill,
In fumes of burning Chocolate shall glow,
And tremble at the sea that froths below !
    He spoke ; the spirits from the sails descend ;
Some, orb in orb, around the nymph extend ;

Some thrid the mazy ringlets of her hair;
Some hang upon the pendants of her ear:
With beating hearts the dire event they wait,
Anxious, and trembling for the birth of Fate.

From CANTO III

OH thoughtless mortals! ever blind to fate,
Too soon dejected, and too soon elate.
Sudden, these honours[1] shall be snatch'd away,
And curs'd for ever this victorious day.
　For lo! the board with cups and spoons is crown'd,
The berries crackle, and the mill turns round;
On shining Altars of Japan they raise
The silver lamp; the fiery spirits blaze:
From silver spouts the grateful liquors glide,
While China's earth receives the smoking tide:
At once they gratify their scent and taste,
And frequent cups prolong the rich repast.
Straight hover round the Fair her airy band;
Some, as she sipp'd, the fuming liquor fann'd,
Some o'er her lap their careful plumes display'd,
Trembling, and conscious of the rich brocade.
Coffee, (which makes the politician wise,
And see thro' all things with his half-shut eyes)
Sent up in vapours to the Baron's brain
New Stratagems, the radiant Lock to gain.
Ah cease, rash youth! desist ere 'tis too late,
Fear the just Gods, and think of Scylla's Fate!
Chang'd to a bird, and sent to flit in air,
She dearly pays for Nisus' injur'd hair!
　But when to mischief mortals bend their will,
How soon they find fit instruments of ill!
Just then, Clarissa drew with tempting grace
A two-edg'd weapon from her shining case:
So Ladies in Romance assist their Knight,
Present the spear, and arm him for the fight.
He takes the gift with rev'rence, and extends
The little engine on his fingers' ends;

[1] The victory at Ombre.

This just behind Belinda's neck he spread,
As o'er the fragrant steams she bends her head.
Swift to the Lock a thousand Sprites repair,
A thousand wings, by turns, blow back the hair;
And thrice they twitch'd the diamond in her ear;
Thrice she look'd back, and thrice the foe drew near.
Just in that instant, anxious Ariel sought
The close recesses of the Virgin's thought;
As on the nosegay in her breast reclin'd,
He watch'd th' Ideas rising in her mind,
Sudden he view'd, in spite of all her art,
An earthly Lover lurking at her heart.
Amaz'd, confus'd, he found his pow'r expir'd,
Resign'd to fate, and with a sigh retir'd.
   The Peer now spreads the glittering Forfex wide,
T' inclose the Lock; now joins it, to divide.
Ev'n then, before the fatal engine clos'd,
A wretched Sylph too fondly interpos'd;
Fate urg'd the shears, and cut the Sylph in twain,
(But airy substance soon unites again)
The meeting points the sacred hair dissever
From the fair head, for ever, and for ever!
   Then flash'd the living lightning from her eyes,
And screams of horror rend th' affrighted skies.
Not louder shrieks to pitying heav'n are cast,
When husbands, or when lapdogs, breathe their last;
Or when rich China vessels fall'n from high,
In glitt'ring dust and painted fragments lie!
   Let wreaths of triumph now my temples twine,
(The victor cry'd) the glorious Prize is mine!
While fish in streams, or birds delight in air,
Or in a coach and six the British Fair,
As long as Atalantis shall be read,
Or the small pillow grace a Lady's bed,
While visits shall be paid on solemn days,
When num'rous wax-lights in bright order blaze,
While nymphs take treats, or assignations give,
So long my honour, name, and praise shall live!

What Time would spare, from Steel receives its date,
And monuments, like men, submit to Fate!
Steel could the labour of the Gods destroy,
And strike to dust th' imperial tow'rs of Troy;
Steel could the works of mortal pride confound,
And hew triumphal arches to the ground.
What wonder then, fair nymph! thy hairs should feel,
The conquering force of unresisted steel?

From Canto IV

BELINDA burns with more than mortal ire,
And fierce Thalestris fans the rising fire.
" O wretched maid! " she spread her hands, and cry'd,
(While Hampton's echoes, " Wretched maid! "
    reply'd)
" Was it for this you took such constant care
The bodkin, comb, and essence to prepare?
For this your locks in paper durance bound,
For this with tort'ring irons wreath'd around?
For this with fillets strain'd your tender head,
And bravely bore the double loads of lead?
Gods! shall the ravisher display your hair,
While the Fops envy, and the Ladies stare!
Honour forbid! at whose unrivall'd shrine
Ease, pleasure, virtue, all our sex resign.
Methinks already I your tears survey,
Already hear the horrid things they say,
Already see you a degraded toast,
And all your honour in a whisper lost!
How shall I, then, your helpless fame defend?
'Twill then be infamy to seem your friend!
And shall this prize, th' inestimable prize,
Expos'd thro' crystal to the gazing eyes,
And heighten'd by the diamond's circling rays,
On that rapacious hand for ever blaze?
Sooner shall grass in Hyde-park Circus grow,
And wits take lodgings in the sound of Bow;
Sooner let earth, air, sea, to Chaos fall,
Men, monkeys, lap-dogs, parrots, perish all! "

She said; then raging to Sir Plume repairs,
And bids her Beau demand the precious hairs:
(Sir Plume of amber snuff-box justly vain,
And the nice conduct of a clouded cane)
With earnest eyes, and round unthinking face,
He first the snuff-box open'd, then the case,
And thus broke out—" My Lord, why, what the devil?
" Z—ds! damn the lock! 'fore Gad, you must be civil!
" Plague on't! 'tis past a jest—nay prithee, pox!
" Give her the hair "—he spoke, and rapp'd his box.
　" It grieves me much " (reply'd the Peer again)
" Who speaks so well should ever speak in vain.
But by this Lock, this sacred Lock I swear,
(Which never more shall join its parted hair;
Which never more its honours shall renew,
Clipp'd from the lovely head where late it grew)
That while my nostrils draw the vital air,
This hand, which won it, shall for ever wear."
He spoke, and speaking, in proud triumph spread
The long-contended honours of her head.

From Canto V

　Some thought it mounted to the Lunar sphere,
Since all things lost on earth are treasur'd there.
There Hero's wits are kept in pond'rous vases,
And beau's in snuff-boxes and tweezer-cases.
There broken vows and death-bed alms are found,
And lovers' hearts with ends of riband bound,
The courtier's promises, and sick man's prayers,
The smiles of harlots, and the tears of heirs,
Cages for gnats, and chains to yoke a flea,
Dry'd butterflies, and tomes of casuistry.
　But trust the Muse—she saw it upward rise,
Tho' mark'd by none but quick, poetic eyes:
(So Rome's great founder to the heav'ns withdrew,
To Proculus alone confess'd in view)
A sudden Star, it shot thro' liquid air,
And drew behind a radiant trail of hair.

Not Berenice's Locks first rose so bright,
The heav'ns bespangling with dishevell'd light.
The Sylphs behold it kindling as it flies,
And pleas'd pursue its progress thro' the skies.
 This the Beau monde shall from the Mall survey,
And hail with music its propitious ray.
This the blest Lover shall for Venus take,
And send up vows from Rosamonda's lake.
This Partridge soon shall view in cloudless skies,
When next he looks thro' Galileo's eyes;
And hence th' egregious wizard shall foredoom
The fate of Louis, and the fall of Rome.
 Then cease, bright Nymph! to mourn thy ravish'd hair,
Which adds new glory to the shining sphere!
Not all the tresses that fair head can boast,
Shall draw such envy as the Lock you lost.
For, after all the murders of your eye,
When, after millions slain, yourself shall die:
When those fair suns shall set, as set they must,
And all those tresses shall be laid in dust,
This Lock, the Muse shall consecrate to fame,
And 'midst the stars inscribe Belinda's name.

ELOISA TO ABELARD

Argument

ABELARD and Eloisa flourished in the twelfth Century; they were two of the most distinguished Persons of their age in learning and beauty, but for nothing more famous than for their unfortunate passion. After a long course of calamities, they retired each to a several Convent, and consecrated the remainder of their days to religion. It was many years after this separation, that a letter of Abelard's to a Friend, which contained the history of his misfortune, fell into the hands of Eloisa. This awakening all her Tenderness, occasioned those celebrated letters (out of which the following is partly extracted) which gives so lively a picture of the struggles of grace and nature, virtue and passion. P.

 IN these deep solitudes and awful cells,
 Where heav'nly-pensive contemplation dwells,

And ever-musing melancholy reigns ;
What means this tumult in a Vestal's veins ?
Why rove my thoughts beyond this last retreat ?
Why feels my heart its long-forgotten heat ?
Yet, yet I love !—From Abelard it came,
And Eloïsa yet must kiss the name.
   Dear fatal name ! rest ever unreveal'd,
Nor pass these lips in holy silence seal'd :
Hide it, my heart, within that close disguise,
Where mix'd with God's, his lov'd Idea lies :
O write it not, my hand—the name appears
Already written—wash it out, my tears !
In vain lost Eloïsa weeps and prays,
Her heart still dictates, and her hand obeys. . . .
   Canst thou forget that sad, that solemn day,
When victims at yon altar's foot we lay ?
Canst thou forget what tears that moment fell,
When, warm in youth, I bade the world farewell ?
As with cold lips I kiss'd the sacred veil,
The shrines all trembled, and the lamps grew pale :
Heav'n scarce believ'd the Conquest it survey'd,
And Saints with wonder heard the vows I made.
Yet then, to those dread altars as I drew,
Not on the Cross my eyes were fixed, but you :
Not grace, or zeal, love only was my call,
And if I lose thy love, I lose my all.
Come ! with thy looks, thy words, relieve my woe,
Those still at least are left thee to bestow.
Still on that breast enamour'd let me lie,
Still drink delicious poison from thy eye,
Pant on thy lip, and to thy heart be press'd ;
Give all thou canst—and let me dream the rest.
Ah no ! instruct me other joys to prize,
With other beauties charm my partial eyes,
Full in my view set all the bright abode,
And make my soul quit Abelard for God.
   Ah, think at least thy flock deserves thy care,
Plants of thy hand, and children of thy pray'r.

From the false world in early youth they fled,
By thee to mountains, wilds, and deserts led.
You rais'd these hallow'd walls; the desert smil'd,
And Paradise was open'd in the Wild.
No weeping orphan saw his father's stores
Our shrines irradiate, or emblaze the floors;
No silver saints, by dying misers giv'n,
Here brib'd the rage of ill-requited heav'n:
But such plain roofs as Piety could raise,
And only vocal with the Maker's praise.
In these lone walls (their days eternal bound)
These moss-grown domes with spiry turrets crown'd,
Where awful arches make a noon-day night,
And the dim windows shed a solemn light;
Thy eyes diffus'd a reconciling ray,
And gleams of glory brighten'd all the day.
But now no face divine contentment wears
'Tis all blank sadness, or continual tears.
See how the force of others pray'rs I try,
(O pious fraud of am'rous charity!)
But why should I on others' pray'rs depend?
Come thou, my father, brother, husband, friend!
Ah let thy handmaid, sister, daughter move,
And all those tender names in one, thy love!
The darksome pines that o'er yon rocks reclin'd
Wave high, and murmur to the hollow wind,
The wand'ring streams that shine between the hills,
The grots that echo to the tinkling rills,
The dying gales that pant upon the trees,
The lakes that quiver to the curling breeze;
No more these scenes my meditation aid,
Or lull to rest the visionary maid.
But o'er the twilight groves and dusky caves,
Long-sounding aisles, and intermingled graves,
Black Melancholy sits, and round her throws
A death-like silence, and a dead repose:
Her gloomy presence saddens all the scene,
Shades ev'ry flow'r, and darkens ev'ry green,

Deepens the murmur of the falling floods,
And breathes a browner horror on the woods.
    Yet here for ever, ever must I stay;
Sad proof how well a lover can obey!
Death, only death, can break the lasting chain:
And here, ev'n then, shall my cold dust remain,
Here all its frailties, all its flames resign,
And wait till 'tis no sin to mix with thine.
    Ah wretch! believ'd the spouse of God in vain,
Confess'd within the slave of love and man.
Assist me, heav'n! but whence arose that pray'r?
Sprung it from piety, or from despair?
Ev'n here, where frozen chastity retires,
Love finds an altar for forbidden fires.
I ought to grieve, but cannot what I ought;
I mourn the lover, not lament the fault;
I view my crime, but kindle at the view,
Repent old pleasures, and solicit new;
Now turn'd to heav'n, I weep my past offence,
Now think of thee, and curse my innocence.
Of all affliction taught a lover yet,
'Tis sure the hardest science to forget!
How shall I lose the sin, yet keep the sense,
And love th' offender, yet detest th' offence?
How the dear object from the crime remove,
Or how distinguish penitence from love?
Unequal task! a passion to resign,
For hearts so touch'd, so pierc'd, so lost as mine.
Ere such a soul regains its peaceful state,
How often must it love, how often hate!
How often hope, despair, resent, regret,
Conceal, disdain,—do all things but forget.
But let heav'n seize it, all at once 'tis fir'd:
Not touch'd, but rapt; not waken'd, but inspir'd!
Oh come! oh teach me nature to subdue,
Renounce my love, my life, myself—and you.
Fill my fond heart with God alone, for he
Alone can rival, can succeed to thee.

THE ESSAY ON MAN
From EPISTLE I

Hope humbly then ; with trembling pinions soar ;
Wait the great teacher Death ; and God adore.
What future bliss, he gives not thee to know,
But gives that Hope to be thy blessing now.
Hope springs eternal in the human breast :
Man never Is, but always To be blest :
The soul, uneasy and confin'd from home,
Rests and expatiates in a life to come.
  Lo, the poor Indian ! whose untutor'd mind
Sees God in clouds, or hears him in the wind ;
His soul, proud Science never taught to stray
Far as the solar walk, or milky way ;
Yet simple Nature to his hope has giv'n,
Behind the cloud-topt hill, an humbler heav'n ;
Some safer world in depth of woods embrac'd,
Some happier island in the watry waste,
Where slaves once more their native land behold,
No fiends torment, no Christians thirst for gold.
To Be, contents his natural desire,
He asks no Angel's wing, no Seraph's fire ;
But thinks, admitted to that equal sky,
His faithful dog shall bear him company. . . .
  All are but parts of one stupendous whole,
Whose body Nature is, and God the soul,
That, chang'd thro' all, and yet in all the same ;
Great in the earth, as in th' ethereal frame ;
Warms in the sun, refreshes in the breeze,
Glows in the stars, and blossoms in the trees,
Lives thro' all life, extends thro' all extent,
Spreads undivided, operates unspent ;
Breathes in our soul, informs our mortal part,
As full, as perfect, in a hair as heart :
As full, as perfect, in vile Man that mourns,
As the rapt Seraph that adores and burns.
To him no high, no low, no great, no small ;
He fills, he bounds, connects, and equals all.

Cease then, nor ORDER Imperfection name :
Our proper bliss depends on what we blame.
Know thy own point : This kind, this due degree
Of blindness, weakness, Heav'n bestows on thee.
Submit.—In this, or any other sphere,
Secure to be as blest as thou canst bear :
Safe in the hand of one disposing Pow'r,
Or in the natal, or the mortal hour.
All Nature is but Art, unknown to thee ;
All Chance, Direction, which thou canst not see ;
All Discord, Harmony not understood ;
All partial Evil, universal Good :
And, spite of Pride, in erring Reason's spite,
One truth is clear, WHATEVER IS, IS RIGHT.

From EPISTLE II

KNOW then thyself, presume not God to scan ;
The proper study of Mankind is Man.
Plac'd on this isthmus of a middle state,
A Being darkly wise, and rudely great :
With too much knowledge for the Sceptic side,
With too much weakness for the Stoic's pride,
He hangs between ; in doubt to act, or rest ;
In doubt to deem himself a God, or beast ;
In doubt his Mind or Body to prefer ;
Born but to die, and reas'ning but to err ;
Alike in ignorance, his reason such,
Whether he thinks too little, or too much :
Chaos of Thought and Passion, all confus'd ;
Still by himself abus'd, or disabus'd ;
Created half to rise, and half to fall ;
Great lord of all things, yet a prey to all ;
Sole judge of Truth, in endless Error hurl'd
The glory, jest, and riddle of the world !

From MORAL ESSAYS

But what are these to great Atossa's[1] mind?
Scarce once herself, by turns all Womankind!
Who, with herself, or others, from her birth
Finds all her life one warfare upon earth:
Shines in exposing Knaves, and painting Fools,
Yet is, whate'er she hates and ridicules.
No Thought advances, but her Eddy Brain
Whisks it about, and down it goes again.
Full sixty years the World has been her Trade,
The wisest Fool much Time has ever made.
From loveless youth to unrespected age,
No Passion gratify'd except her Rage.
So much the Fury still out-ran the Wit,
The Pleasure miss'd her, and the Scandal hit.
Who breaks with her, provokes Revenge from Hell,
But he's a bolder man who dares be well.
Her ev'ry turn with Violence pursu'd,
Nor more a storm her Hate than Gratitude:
To that each Passion turns, or soon or late;
Love, if it makes her yield, must make her hate:
Superiors? death! and Equals? what a curse!
But an Inferior not dependant? worse.
Offend her, and she knows not to forgive;
Oblige her, and she'll hate you while you live;
But die, and she'll adore you—Then the Bust
And Temple rise—then fall again to dust.
Last night, her Lord was all that's good and great;
A Knave this morning, and his Will a Cheat.
Strange! by the Means defeated of the Ends,
By Spirit robb'd of Pow'r, by Warmth of Friends,
By Wealth of Follow'rs! without one distress
Sick of herself thro' very selfishness!
Atossa, curs'd with ev'ry granted pray'r,
Childless with all her Children, wants an Heir.
To Heirs unknown, descends th' unguarded store,
Or wanders heaven-directed, to the poor. . . .

[1] Duchess of Marlborough.

Pleasures the sex, as children Birds, pursue,
Still out of reach, yet never out of view ;
Sure, if they catch, to spoil the Toy at most,
To covet flying, and regret when lost :
At last, to follies Youth could scarce defend,
It grows their Age's prudence to pretend ;
Asham'd to own they gave delight before,
Reduc'd to feign it, when they give no more :
As Hags hold Sabbaths, less for joy than spite,
So these their merry, miserable Night ;
Still round and round the ghosts of Beauty glide,
And haunt the places where their Honour died.
　See how the World its Veterans rewards !
A Youth of Frolics, an old Age of Cards ;
Fair to no purpose, artful to no end,
Young without Lovers, old without a Friend ;
A Fop their Passion, but their Prize a Sot ;
Alive, ridiculous, and dead, forgot !

From THE EPISTLE TO DR. ARBUTHNOT

P. SHUT, shut the door, good John ! fatigu'd, I said,
Tie up the knocker, say I'm sick, I'm dead.
The Dog-star rages ! nay 'tis past a doubt,
All Bedlam, or Parnassus, is let out :
Fire in each eye, and papers in each hand,
They rave, recite, and madden round the land.
　What walls can guard me, or what shades can hide ?
They pierce my thickets, thro' my Grot they glide ;
By land, by water, they renew the charge ;
They stop the chariot, and they board the barge.
No place is sacred, not the Church is free ;
Ev'n Sunday shines no Sabbath-day to me ;
Then from the Mint walks forth the Man of rhyme,
Happy to catch me just at Dinner-time.
　Is there a Parson, much bemus'd in beer,
A maudlin Poetess, a rhyming Peer,
A Clerk, foredoom'd his father's soul to cross,
Who pens a Stanza, when he should *engross* ?

ALEXANDER POPE

Is there, who, lock'd from ink and paper, scrawls
With desp'rate charcoal round his darken'd walls?
All fly to TWIT'NAM, and in humble strain
Apply to me, to keep them mad or vain.
Arthur, whose giddy son neglects the Laws,
Imputes to me and my damn'd works the cause:
Poor Cornus sees his frantic wife elope,
And curses Wit, and Poetry, and Pope.
   Friend to my Life! (which did not you prolong,
The world had wanted many an idle song)
What *Drop* or *Nostrum* can this plague remove?
Or which must end me, a Fool's wrath or love?
A dire dilemma! either way I'm sped,
If foes, they write, if friends, they read me dead.
Seiz'd and tied down to judge, how wretched I!
Who can't be silent, and who will not lie.
To laugh, were want of goodness and of grace,
And to be grave, exceeds all Pow'r of face.
I sit with sad civility, I read
With honest anguish, and an aching head;
And drop at last, but in unwilling ears,
This saving counsel, " Keep your piece nine years." . . .
If I dislike it, " Furies, death and rage! "
If I approve, " Commend it to the Stage."
There (thank my stars) my whole Commission ends,
The Play'rs and I are, luckily, no friends,
Fir'd that the house reject him, " 'Sdeath I'll print it,
And shame the fools——Your Int'rest, Sir, with
    Lintot! "
" Lintot, dull rogue! will think your price too much:"
" Not, sir, if you revise it, and retouch."
All my demurs but double his Attacks;
At last he whispers, " Do; and we go snacks."
Glad of a quarrel, straight I clap the door,
Sir, let me see your works and you no more. . . .
   Why did I write? what sin to me unknown
Dipt me in ink, my parents', or my own?
As yet a child, nor yet a fool to fame,
I lisp'd in numbers, for the numbers came.

I left no calling for this idle trade,
No duty broke, no father disobey'd.
The Muse but serv'd to ease some friend, not Wife,
To help me thro' this long disease, my Life,
To second, ARBUTHNOT! thy Art and Care,
And teach the Being you preserv'd, to bear.
    But why then publish? *Granville* the polite,
And knowing *Walsh*, would tell me I could write;
Well-natur'd *Garth* inflam'd with early praise;
And *Congreve* lov'd, and *Swift* endur'd my lays;
Thè courtly *Talbot, Somers, Sheffield* read;
Ev'n mitred *Rochester* would nod the head,
And *St. John's* self (great *Dryden's* friends before)
With open arms receiv'd one Poet more.
Happy my studies, when by these approv'd!
Happier their author, when by these belov'd!
From these the world will judge of men and books,
Not from the *Burnets, Oldmixons,* and *Cookes.*
    Soft were my numbers; who could take offence,
While pure Description held the place of Sense?
Like gentle *Fanny's* was my flow'ry theme,
A painted mistress, or a purling stream.
Yet then did *Gildon* draw his venal quill;—
I wish'd the man a dinner, and sat still.
Yet then did *Dennis* rave in furious fret;
I never answer'd,—I was not in debt.
If want provok'd, or madness made them print,
I wag'd no war with *Bedlam* or the *Mint.*
    Did some more sober Critic come abroad;
If wrong, I smil'd; if right, I kiss'd the rod.
Pains, reading, study, are their just pretence,
And all they want is spirit, taste, and sense.
Commas and points they set exactly right,
And 'twere a sin to rob them of their mite.
Yet ne'er one sprig of laurel grac'd these ribalds,
From slashing *Bentley* down to pidling *Tibalds.*
Each wight, who reads not, and but scans and spells,
Each Word-catcher, that lives on syllables,

Ev'n such small Critics some regard may claim,
Preserv'd in *Milton's* or in *Shakespeare's* name.
Pretty! in amber to observe the forms
Of hairs, or straws, or dirt, or grubs, or worms!
The things, we know, are neither rich nor rare,
But wonder how the devil they got there.
   Were others angry: I excus'd them too;
Well might they rage, I gave them but their due.
A man's true merit 'tis not hard to find;
But each man's secret standard in his mind,
That Casting-weight pride adds to emptiness,
This, who can gratify? for who can *guess*?
The Bard whom pilfer'd Pastorals renown,
Who turns a Persian tale for half a Crown,
Just writes to make his barrenness appear,
And strains, from hard-bound brains, eight lines a year;
He, who still wanting, tho' he lives on theft,
Steals much, spends little, yet has nothing left.
And He, who now to sense, now nonsense leaning,
Means not, but blunders round about a meaning.
And He, whose fustian's so sublimely bad,
It is not Poetry, but prose run mad.
All these, my modest Satire bade *translate*,
And own'd that nine such Poets made a *Tate*.
How did they fume, and stamp, and roar, and chafe!
And swear, not ADDISON himself was safe.
   Peace to all such! but were there One whose fires
True Genius kindles, and fair Fame inspires;
Blest with each talent and each art to please,
And born to write, converse, and live with ease:
Should such a man, too fond to rule alone,
Bear, like the Turk, no brother near the throne.
View him with scornful, yet with jealous eyes,
And hate for arts that caus'd himself to rise;
Damn with faint praise, assent with civil leer,
And without sneering, teach the rest to sneer;
Willing to wound, and yet afraid to strike,
Just hint a fault, and hesitate dislike;

Alike reserv'd to blame, or to commend,
A tim'rous foe, and a suspicious friend;
Dreading ev'n fools, by Flatterers besieg'd,
And so obliging, that he ne'er oblig'd;
Like *Cato*, give his little Senate laws,
And sit attentive to his own applause;
While Wits and Templars ev'ry sentence raise,
And wonder with a foolish face of praise:——
Who but must laugh, if such a man there be?
Who would not weep, if ATTICUS[1] were he? . . .
    Let *Sporus* tremble[2]— *A.* What? that thing of silk,
Sporus, that mere white curd of Ass's milk?
Satire or sense, alas! can *Sporus* feel?
Who breaks a butterfly upon a wheel?
P. Yet let me flap this bug with gilded wings,
This painted child of dirt, that stinks and stings;
Whose buzz the witty and the fair annoys,
Yet wit ne'er tastes, and beauty ne'er enjoys:
So well-bred spaniels civilly delight
In mumbling of the game they dare not bite.
Eternal smiles his emptiness betray,
As shallow streams run dimpling all the way.
Whether in florid impotence he speaks,
And, as the prompter breathes, the puppet squeaks;
Or at the ear of *Eve*, familiar Toad,
Half froth, half venom, spits himself abroad,
In puns, or politics, or tales, or lies,
Or spite, or smut, or rhymes, or blasphemies.
His wit all see-saw, between *that* and *this*,
Now high, now low, now master up, now miss,
And he himself one vile Antithesis.
Amphibious thing! that acting either part,
The trifling head or the corrupted heart,
Fop at the toilet, flatt'rer at the board,
Now trips a Lady, and now struts a Lord.
Eve's tempter thus the Rabbins have exprest,
A Cherub's face, a reptile all the rest;

    [1] Addison.   [2] John Lord Hervey.

Beauty that shocks you, parts that none will trust;
Wit that can creep, and pride that licks the dust.
  Not Fortune's worshipper, nor fashion's fool,
Not Lucre's madman, nor Ambition's tool,
Not proud, nor servile;—be one Poet's praise,
That, if he pleas'd, he pleas'd by manly ways:
That Flatt'ry, ev'n to Kings, he held a shame,
And thought a Lie in verse or prose the same.
That not in Fancy's maze he wander'd long,
But stoop'd to Truth, and moraliz'd his song:
That not for Fame, but Virtue's better end,
He stood the furious foe, the timid friend,
The damning critic, half approving wit,
The coxcomb hit, or fearing to be hit;
Laugh'd at the loss of friends he never had,
The dull, the proud, the wicked, and the mad;
The distant threats of vengeance on his head,
The blow unfelt, the tear he never shed;
The tale reviv'd, the lie so oft o'erthrown,
Th' imputed trash, and dulness not his own;
The morals blacken'd when the writings scape,
The libell'd person, and the pictur'd shape;
Abuse, on all he lov'd, or lov'd him, spread,
A friend in exile, or a father, dead;
The whisper, that to greatness still too near,
Perhaps, yet vibrates on his Sov'REIGN's ear:—
Welcome for thee, fair *Virtue*! all the past;
For thee, fair Virtue! welcome ev'n the *last*!

HENRY CAREY (d. 1743)
SALLY IN OUR ALLEY

  OF all the girls that are so smart
    There's none like pretty Sally,
  She is the Darling of my Heart,
    And she lives in our Alley.
  There is no Lady in the Land
    Is half so sweet as Sally,
  She is the Darling of my Heart,
    And she lives in our Alley.

Her father he makes Cabbage-nets,
    And through the Streets does cry 'em;
Her Mother she sells Laces long,
    To such as please to buy 'em:
But sure such Folks could ne'er beget
    So sweet a Girl as Sally!
She is the Darling of my Heart,
    And she lives in our Alley.

When she is by, I leave my Work,
    (I love her so sincerely)
My Master comes like any Turk,
    And bangs me most severely;
But let him bang his Bellyful,
    I'll bear it all for Sally;
She is the Darling of my Heart,
    And she lives in our Alley.

Of all the Days that's in the Week,
    I dearly love but one Day,
And that's the day that comes betwixt
    A Saturday and Monday;
For then I'm drest, all in my best,
    To walk abroad with Sally;
She is the Darling of my Heart,
    And she lives in our Alley.

My master carries me to Church,
    And often am I blamed,
Because I leave him in the lurch,
    As soon as Text is named:
I leave the Church in Sermon time,
    And slink away to Sally;
She is the Darling of my Heart,
    And she lives in our Alley.

When Christmas comes about again,
    O then I shall have Money;
I'll hoard it up, and Box and all
    I'll give it to my Honey:

And, would it were ten thousand Pounds;
  I'd give it all to Sally;
She is the Darling of my Heart,
  And she lives in our Alley.

My Master and the Neighbours all,
  Make game of me and Sally;
And (but for her) I'd better be
  A Slave and row a Galley:
But when my seven long Years are out,
  O then I'll marry Sally!
O then we'll wed and then we'll bed,
  But not in our Alley.

SAMUEL WESLEY THE YOUNGER
(1691–1739)

FROM A HINT IN THE MINOR POETS

No! not for Those of Women born
  Not so unlike the Die is cast;
For, after all our Vaunt and Scorn,
  How very small the Odds at last!

Him, rais'd to Fortune's utmost Top,
  With Him beneath her Feet compare;
And One has nothing more to hope,
  And One has nothing more to fear.

JOHN BYROM (1692–1763)

A PASTORAL

My Time, O ye Muses, was happily spent,
When *Phebe* went with me wherever I went;
Ten thousand sweet Pleasures I felt in my Breast:
Sure never fond Shepherd like *Colin* was blest!
But now she is gone, and has left me behind,
What a marvellous Change on a sudden I find!
When Things were as fine as could possibly be,
I thought 'twas the Spring; but alas! it was she.

With such a Companion to tend a few Sheep,
To rise up and play, or to lie down and sleep:
I was so good humour'd, so cheerful and gay,
My Heart was as light as a Feather all Day.
But now I so cross, and so peevish am grown,
So strangely uneasy, as never was known.
My fair one is gone, and my joys are all drown'd,
And my Heart—I am sure, it weighs more than a
    Pound. . . .

When walking with *Phebe*, what sights I have seen!
How fair was the Flower, how fresh was the Green!
What a lovely Appearance the Trees and the Shade,
The Corn-fields and Hedges, and ev'ry Thing made!
But now she has left me, tho' all are still there,
They none of them now so delightful appear:
'Twas naught but the Magic, I find, of her Eyes
Made so many beautiful Prospects arise.

Sweet Music went with us both all the Wood through,
The Lark, Linnet, Throstle, and Nightingale too;
Winds over us whisper'd, Flocks by us did Bleat,
And chirp went the Grasshopper under our Feet.
But now she is absent, though still they sing on,
The Woods are but lonely, the Melody's gone:
Her Voice in the Consort, as now I have found,
Gave ev'ry Thing else its agreeable Sound.

Rose what is become of thy delicate Hue?
And where is the Violet's beautiful Blue?
Does ought of its Sweetness the Blossom beguile?
That Meadow, those Daisies, why do they not smile?
Ah! Rivals, I see what it was that you dressed,
And made yourselves fine for—a Place in her Breast:
You put on your Colours to pleasure her Eye,
To be plucked by her Hand, on her Bosom to die.

How slowly Time creeps, till my *Phebe* return!
While amidst the soft Zephyr's cold Breezes I burn;
Methinks if I knew whereabouts he would tread,
I could breathe on his Wings, and 'twould melt down
  the Lead.
Fly swifter, ye Minutes, bring hither my Dear,
And rest so much longer for't when she is here.
Ah, *Colin*! old Time is full of delay,
Nor will budge one Foot faster for all thou canst say.

Will no pitying Pow'r, that hears me complain,
Or cure my disquiet, or soften my pain?
To be cur'd, thou must, *Colin*, thy passion remove;
But what swain is so silly to live without love?
No, Deity, bid the dear Nymph to return,
For ne'er was poor Shepherd so sadly forlorn.
Ah! what shall I do? I shall die with despair;
Take heed, all ye Swains, how ye part with your Fair.

PHILIP STANHOPE, EARL OF CHESTERFIELD (1694–1773)

VERSES WRITTEN IN A LADY'S "SHERLOCK [1] UPON DEATH"

    Mistaken fair, lay Sherlock by,
      His doctrine is deceiving;
    For whilst he teaches us to die,
      He cheats us of our living.

    To die's a lesson we shall know
      Too soon, without a master;
    Then let us only study now
      How we may live the faster.

    To live's to love, to bless, be blest
      With mutual inclination;
    Share then my ardour in your breast,
      And kindly meet my passion.

[1] William Sherlock's *A Practical Discourse concerning Death.* 1692.

> But if thus bless'd I may not live,
>   And pity you deny,
> To me at least your Sherlock give,
>   'Tis I must learn to die.

ANONYMOUS (1731)
SONG

As swift as Time put round the Glass,
And husband well Life's little Space;
Perhaps your Sun which shines so bright,
May set in everlasting Night.

Or if the Sun again should rise,
Death, ere the Morn, may close our Eyes,
Then drink before it be too late,
And snatch the present Hour from Fate.

Come, fill a Bumper, fill it round
Let Mirth and Wit and Wine abound;
In these alone True Wisdom lies,
For to be Merry's to be Wise.

MATTHEW GREEN (1696–1737)
From THE SPLEEN

This motley piece to you I send,
Who always were a faithful friend,
Who, if disputes should happen hence,
Can best explain the author's sense,
And, anxious for the public weal,
Do, what I sing, so often feel.
  The want of method pray excuse,
Allowing for a vapour'd Muse;
Nor, to a narrow path confin'd,
Hedge in by rules a roving mind.
  The child is genuine, you can trace,
Throughout, the fire's transmitted face.

Nothing is stolen : my Muse, though mean,
Draws from the spring, she finds within ;
Nor vainly buys, what Gildon sells,
Poetic buckets for dry wells.

．　　．　　．　　．

   First know, my friend, I do not mean
To write a treatise on the spleen ;
Nor to prescribe, when nerves convulse,
Nor mend th' alarum watch, your pulse :
If I am right, your question lay,
What course I take to drive away
The day-mare spleen, by whose false pleas
Men prove mere suicides in ease ;
And how I do myself demean
In stormy world to live serene. . . .
   That tribe, whose practicals decree
Small-beer the deadliest heresy ;
Who, fond of pedigree, derive
From the most noted whore alive,
Who own wine's old prophetic aid,
And love the mitre Bacchus made,
Forbid the faithful to depend
On half-pint drinkers for a friend ;
And in whose gay red-letter'd face
We read good-living more than grace :
Nor they so pure, and so precise,
Immac'late as their white of eyes ;
Who for the spirit hug the Spleen
Phylacter'd throughout all their mien ;
Who their ill-tasted home-brew'd prayer
To the state's mellow forms prefer ;
Who doctrines, as infectious, fear,
Which are not steep'd in vinegar ;
And samples of heart-chested grace
Expose in shew-glass of the face ;
Did never me as yet provoke,
Either to honour band and cloak,
Or deck my hat with leaves of oak.

I rail not with mock-patriot grace
At folks, because they are in place,
Nor, hir'd to praise with stallion pen
Serve the ear-lechery of men;
But to avoid religious jars
The laws are my expositors,
Which in my doubting mind create
Conformity to church and state.
I go, pursuant to my plan,
To Mecca with the caravan,
And think it right in common sense
Both for diversion and defence.
   Reforming schemes are none of mine,
To mend the world's a vast design,
Like theirs, who tug in little boat
To pull to them the ship afloat,
While, to defeat their labour'd end,
At once both wind and stream contend:
Success herein is seldom seen,
And zeal, when baffled, turns to spleen.
   Happy the man, who innocent
Grieves not at ills, he can't prevent;
His skiff does with the current glide,
Not puffing pull'd against the tide;
He, paddling by the scuffling crowd,
Sees unconcern'd life's wager row'd,
And when he can't prevent foul-play,
Enjoys the folly of the fray. . . .
The fabled goods, the poets sing,
A season of perpetual spring,
Brooks, flow'ry fields, and groves of trees
Affording sweets, and similes,
Gay dreams inspir'd in myrtle bowers,
And wreaths of undecaying flowers,
Apollo's harp with airs divine,
The sacred music of the nine,
Views of the temple rais'd to fame,
And for a vacant niche proud aim
Ravish their souls, and plainly show,

What fancy's sketching pow'r can do;
They will attempt the mountain steep,
Where on the top, like dreams in sleep,
The Muses revelations show,
That find men cracked, or make them so.
   You friend, like me, the trade of rhyme
Avoid, elaborate waste of time,
Nor are content to be undone,
And pass for Phoebus' crazy son.
Poems, the hop-grounds of the brain,
Afford the most uncertain gain;
And lotteries never tempt the wise,
With blanks so many to a prize.
I only transient visits pay,
Meeting the Muses in my way,
Scarce known to the fastidious dames,
Nor skill'd to call them by their names;
Nor can their passports in these days
Your profit warrant, or your praise:
On poems by their dictates writ
Critics, as sworn appraisers sit,
And, mere upholsterers, in a trice
On gems and paintings set a price;
These Tayl'ring artists for our lays
Invent cramp'd rules, and with strait stays
Striving free nature's shape to hit,
Emaciate sense, before they fit. . . .
   Thus shelter'd free from care and strife,
May I enjoy a calm through life;
See faction, safe in low degree,
As men at land see storms at sea;
And laugh at miserable elves
Not kind, so much as to themselves,
Cursed with such souls of base alloy,
As can possess, but not enjoy.
Debarr'd the pleasure to impart
By avarice, sphincter of the heart,
Who wealth, hard earn'd by guilty cares,
Bequeath untouch'd to thankless heirs.

May I, with look ungloom'd by guile,
And wearing virtue's livery-smile ;
Prone the distressed to relieve,
And little trespasses forgive ;
With income not in fortune's pow'r,
And skill to make a busy hour ;
With trips to town, life to amuse,
To purchase books, and hear the news,
To see old friends, brush off the clown,
And quicken taste at coming down ;
Unhurt by sickness' blasting rage,
And slowly mellowing in age,
When fate extends its gathering gripe
Fall off like fruit grown fully ripe,
Quit a worn being without pain,
Perhaps to blossom soon again. . . .
A stranger into life I'm come,
Dying may be our going home,
Transported here by angry fate,
The convicts of a prior state :
Hence I no anxious thoughts bestow
On matters, I can never know.
Through life's foul ways, like vagrant, pass'd,
He'll grant a settlement at last ;
And with sweet ease the wearied crown,
By leave to lay his being down.
If doom'd to dance th' eternal round
Of life, no sooner lost than found ;
And dissolution soon to come,
Like sponge, wipes out life's present sum,
But can't our state of pow'r bereave
An endless series to receive :
Then if hard dealt with here by fate,
We balance in another state,
And consciousness must go along,
And sign th' acquittance for the wrong ;
He for his creatures must decree
More happiness than misery,
Or to be supposed to create,

Curious to try, what 'tis to hate,
And do an act, which rage infers,
'Cause lameness halts, or blindness errs.
  Thus, thus I steer my bark, and sail
On even keel with gentle gale.
At helm I make my reason sit,
My crew of passions all submit.
If dark and blust'ring prove some nights
Philosophy puts forth her lights;
Experience holds the cautious glass,
To shun the breakers, as I pass;
And frequent throws the wary lead,
To see what dangers may be hid.
And once in seven years I'm seen
At Bath, or Tunbridge to careen.
Tho' pleas'd to see the dolphins play,
I mind my compass and my way;
With store sufficient for relief,
And wisely still prepar'd to reef;
Nor wanting the dispersive bowl
Of cloudy weather in the soul,
I make (may heaven propitious send
Such wind and weather to the end)
Neither becalm'd, nor overblown,
Life's voyage to the world unknown.

JAMES THOMSON (1700–1748)
SONG

UNLESS with my *Amanda* blest
  In vain I twine the woodbine bower;
Unless to deck her sweeter breast,
  In vain I rear the breathing flower:

Awaken'd by the genial year,
  In vain the birds around me sing;
In vain the fresh'ning fields appear:
  Without my love there is no spring.

SELECTIONS FROM *THE SEASONS*

From SPRING

But why so far excursive ? when at hand,
Along these blushing borders, bright with dew,
And in yon mingled wilderness of flowers,
Fair-handed Spring unbosoms every grace :
Throws out the snowdrop and the crocus first ;
The daisy, primrose, violet darkly blue,
And polyanthus of unnumber'd dyes ;
The yellow wallflower, stain'd with iron brown ;
And lavish stock that scents the garden round ;
From the soft wing of vernal breezes shed,
Anemones ; auriculas, enrich'd
With shining meal o'er all their velvet leaves ;
And full ranunculus, of glowing red.
Then comes the tulip-race, where beauty plays
Her idle freaks : from family diffused
To family, as flies the father-dust,
The varied colours run ; and, while they break
On the charm'd eye, the exulting florist marks,
With secret pride, the wonders of his hand.
No gradual bloom is wanting ; from the bud,
First-born of Spring, to Summer's musky tribes :
Nor hyacinths, of purest virgin-white,
Low-bent, and blushing inward ; nor jonquils,
Of potent fragrance ; nor narcissus fair,
As o'er the fabled fountain hanging still ;
Nor broad carnations, nor gay-spotted pinks ;
Nor, showered from every bush, the damask-rose.
Infinite numbers, delicacies, smells,
With hues on hues expression cannot paint,
The breath of Nature, and her endless bloom.

From SUMMER

Confess'd from yonder slow-extinguish'd clouds,
All ether softening, sober evening takes
Her wonted station in the middle air :

A thousand shadows at her beck. First this
She sends on earth ; then that of deeper dye
Steals soft behind ; and then a deeper still,
In circle following circle, gathers round,
To close the face of things. A fresher gale
Begins to wave the wood, and stir the stream,
Sweeping with shadowy gust the fields of corn ;
While the quail clamours for his running mate. . . .

   His folded flock secure, the shepherd home
Hies, merry-hearted ; and by turns relieves
The ruddy milkmaid of her brimming pail ;
The beauty whom perhaps his witless heart,
Unknowing what the joy-mix'd anguish means,
Sincerely loves, by that best language shewn
Of cordial glances and obliging deeds.
Onward they pass, o'er many a panting height,
And valley sunk, and unfrequented ; where
At fall of eve the fairy people throng,
In various game and revelry to pass
The summer-night, as village stories tell. . . .

   Among the crooked lanes, on every hedge,
The glow-worm lights his gem ; and through the dark,
A moving radiance twinkles. Evening yields
The world to night ; not in her winter robe
Of massy Stygian woof, but loose array'd
In mantle dun. A faint erroneous ray,
Glanced from the imperfect surfaces of things,
Flings half an image on the straining eye ;
While wavering woods, and villages, and streams,
And rocks, and mountain-tops, that long retain'd
The ascending gleam, are all one swimming scene,
Uncertain if beheld. Sudden to heaven
Thence weary vision turns ; where, leading soft
The silent hours of love, with purest ray
Sweet Venus shines ; and from her genial rise
When daylight sickens, till it springs afresh,
Unrivall'd reigns, the fairest lamp of night.

From AUTUMN

Thus solitary, and in pensive guise,
Oft let me wander o'er the russet mead,
And through the sadden'd grove, where scarce is heard
One dying strain to cheer the woodman's toil.
Haply some widow'd songster pours his plaint,
Far, in faint warblings, through the tawny copse;
While congregated thrushes, linnets, larks,
And each wild throat, whose artless strains so late
Swell'd all the music of the swarming shades,
Robb'd of their tuneful souls, now shivering sit
On the dead tree, a dull despondent flock!
With not a brightness waving o'er their plumes,
And nought save chattering discord in their note.
Oh! let not, aim'd from some inhuman eye,
The gun, the music of the coming year
Destroy; and harmless, unsuspecting harm,
Lay the weak tribes, a miserable prey,
In mingled murder, fluttering on the ground.
 The pale descending year, yet pleasing still,
A gentler mood inspires; for now the leaf
Incessant rustles from the mournful grove;
Oft startling such as, studious, walk below,
And slowly circles through the waving air.
But should a quicker breeze amid the boughs
Sob, o'er the sky the leafy deluge streams;
Till choked and matted with the dreary shower,
The forest-walks, at every rising gale,
Roll wide the wither'd waste, and whistle bleak.
Fled is the blasted verdure of the fields;
And, shrunk into their beds, the flowery race
Their sunny robes resign. Even what remain'd
Of bolder fruits falls from the naked tree;
And woods, fields, gardens, orchards, all around
The desolated prospect thrills the soul. . . .
 The lengthen'd night elapsed, the morning shines
Serene, in all her dewy beauty bright,
Unfolding fair the last autumnal day.

And now the mounting sun dispels the fog;
The rigid hoar-frost melts before his beam;
And hung on every spray, on every blade
Of grass, the myriad dewdrops twinkle round. . . .

From WINTER

THE keener tempests come: and fuming dun
From all the living east, or piercing north,
Thick clouds ascend, in whose capacious womb
A vapoury deluge lies, to snow congeal'd.
Heavy they roll their fleecy world along;
And the sky saddens with the gather'd storm.
Through the hush'd air the whit'ning shower descends,
At first thin wavering; till at last the flakes
Fall broad, and wide, and fast, dimming the day
With a continual flow. The cherish'd fields
Put on their winter robe of purest white.
'Tis brightness all; save where the new snow melts
Along the mazy current. Low, the woods
Bow their hoar head; and, ere the languid sun
Faint from the west emits his evening ray,
Earth's universal face, deep-hid and chill,
Is one wild dazzling waste, that buries wide
The works of man. Drooping, the labourer-ox
Stands cover'd o'er with snow, and then demands
The fruit of all his toil. The fowls of heaven,
Tamed by the cruel season, crowd around
The winnowing store, and claim the little boon
Which Providence assigns them. One alone,
The redbreast, sacred to the household gods,
Wisely regardful of the embroiling sky,
In joyless fields and thorny thickets leaves
His shivering mates, and pays to trusted man
His annual visit. Half-afraid, he first
Against the window beats; then, brisk, alights
On the warm hearth; then, hopping o'er the floor,
Eyes all the smiling family askance,
And pecks and starts, and wonders where he is;
Till, more familiar grown, the table-crumbs

Attract his slender feet. The foodless wilds
Pour forth their brown inhabitants. The hare,
Though timorous of heart, and hard beset
By death in various forms, dark snares, and dogs,
And more unpitying men, the garden seeks,
Urged on my fearless want. The bleating kind
Eye the black heaven, and next the glistening earth,
With looks of dumb despair; then, sad dispersed,
Dig for the wither'd herb through heaps of snow. . . .
    Meantime the village rouses up the fire:
While, well attested, and as well believed,
Heard solemn, goes the goblin story round,
Till superstitious horror creeps o'er all.
Or, frequent in the sounding hall, they wake
The rural gambol. Rustic mirth goes round:
The simple joke that takes the shepherd's heart,
Easily pleased; the long loud laugh, sincere;
The kiss, snatch'd hasty from the sidelong maid,
On purpose guardless, or pretending sleep;
The leap, the slap, the haul; and, shook to notes
Of native music, the respondent dance.
Thus jocund fleets with them the winter night. . . .

THE CASTLE OF INDOLENCE

ADVERTISEMENT

    This poem being writ in the Manner of *Spenser*, the obsolete Words, and a Simplicity of Diction in some of the Lines, which borders on the Ludicrous, were necessary to make the Imitation more perfect. And the style of that admirable Poet as well as the Measure in which he wrote, are as it were appropriated by Custom to all Allegorical Poems writ in our Language; just as in French the style of *Marot* who lived under *Francis I.* has been used in Tales, and familiar Epistles, by the politest writers of the Age of *Louis XIV.*

Canto I

The Castle hight of Indolence,
  And its false Luxury;
Where for a little Time, alas!
  We liv'd right jollily.

I

O Mortal Man, who livest here by Toil,
Do not complain of this thy hard Estate;
That like an Emmet thou must ever moil,
Is a sad Sentence of an ancient Date:
And, certes, there is for it Reason great;
For, though sometimes it makes thee weep and wail,
And curse thy Star, and early drudge and late,
Withouten That would come an heavier Bale,
Loose Life, unruly Passions, and Diseases pale.

II

In lowly Dale, fast by a River's Side,
With woody Hill o'er Hill encompass'd round,
A most enchanting Wizard did abide,
Than whom a Fiend more fell is no where found.
It was, I ween, a lovely Spot of Ground;
And there a Season atween June and May,
Half prankt with Spring, with Summer half imbrown'd,
A listless Climate made, where, Sooth to say,
No living Wight could work, ne cared even for Play.

III

Was nought around but Images of Rest:
Sleep-soothing Groves, and quiet Lawns between;
And flowery Beds that slumbrous Influence kest,
From Poppies breath'd; and Beds of pleasant Green,
Where never yet was creeping Creature seen.
Meantime unnumber'd glittering Streamlets play'd,
And hurled every-where their Waters sheen;
That, as they bicker'd through the sunny Glade,
Though restless still themselves, a lulling Murmur made.

IV

Join'd to the Prattle of the purling Rills,
Were heard the lowing Herds along the Vale,
And Flocks loud-bleating from the distant Hills,
And vacant Shepherds piping in the Dale;

And now and then sweet Philomel would wail,
Or Stock-Doves plain amid the Forest deep,
That drowsy rustled to the sighing Gale ;
And still a Coil the Grasshopper did keep :
Yet all these Sounds yblent inclined all to Sleep.

V

Full in the Passage of the Vale, above,
A sable, silent, solemn Forest stood ;
Where nought but shadowy Forms were seen to move,
As *Idless* fancy'd in her dreaming Mood.
And up the Hills, on either Side, a Wood
Of blackening Pines, ay waving to and fro,
Sent forth a sleepy Horror through the Blood ;
And where this Valley winded out, below,
The murmuring Main was heard, and scarcely heard, to flow.

VI

A pleasing Land of Drowsy-hed it was :
Of Dreams that wave before the half-shut eye ;
And of gay Castles in the Clouds that pass,
For ever flushing round a Summer-Sky :
There eke the soft Delights, that witchingly
Instil a wanton Sweetness through the Breast,
And the calm Pleasures always hover'd nigh ;
But whate'er smack'd of Noyance, or Unrest,
Was far far off expell'd from this delicious Nest.

VII

The Landskip such, inspiring perfect Ease,
Where *Indolence* (for so the Wizard hight)
Close-hid his Castle mid embowering Trees,
That half shut out the Beams of *Phœbus* bright,
And made a kind of checker'd Day and Night.
Mean while, unceasing at the massy Gate,
Beneath a spacious Palm, the wicked Wight
Was plac'd ; and to his Lute, of cruel Fate,
And Labour harsh, complain'd, lamenting Man's Estate.

VIII

Thither continual Pilgrims crouded still,
From all the Roads of Earth that pass there by:
For, as they chaunc'd to breathe on neighbouring Hill,
The Freshness of this Valley smote their Eye,
And drew them ever and anon more nigh,
'Till clustering round th' Enchanter false they hung,
Ymolten with his Syren Melody;
While o'er th' enfeebling Lute his Hand he flung,
And to the trembling Chords these tempting Verses sung:

IX

"Behold! ye Pilgrims of this Earth, behold!
See all but Man with unearn'd Pleasure gay.
See her bright Robes the Butterfly unfold,
Broke from her wintry Tomb in Prime of May.
What youthful Bride can equal her Array?
Who can with Her for easy Pleasure vie?
From Mead to Mead with gentle Wing to stray,
From Flower to Flower on balmy Gales to fly,
Is all she has to do beneath the radiant Sky.

X

"Behold the merry Minstrels of the Morn,
The swarming Songsters of the careless Grove,
Ten thousand Throats! that, from the flowering Thorn,
Hymn their Good *God*, and carol sweet of Love,
Such grateful kindly Raptures them emove:
They neither plough, nor sow; ne, fit for Flail,
E'er to the Barn the nodding Sheaves they drove;
Yet theirs each Harvest dancing in the Gale,
Whatever crowns the Hill, or smiles along the Vale.

XI

"Outcast of Nature, Man! the wretched Thrall
Of bitter-dropping Sweat, of sweltry Pain,
Of Cares that eat away thy Heart with Gall,
And of the Vices, an inhuman Train,
That all proceed from savage Thirst of Gain:
For when hard-hearted *Interest* first began
To poison earth, *Astræa* left the Plain;
Guile, Violence, and Murder seiz'd on Man;
And, for soft milky Streams, with Blood the Rivers ran.

XII

"Come ye, who still the cumbrous Load of Life
Push hard up Hill; but as the farthest Steep
You trust to gain, and put an End to Strife,
Down thunders back the Stone with mighty Sweep,
And hurls your Labours to the Valley deep,
For-ever vain: come, and, withouten Fee,
I in Oblivion will your Sorrows steep,
Your Cares, your Toils, will steep you in a Sea
Of full Delight: O come, ye weary Wights, to me!

XIII

"With me, you need not rise at early Dawn,
To pass the joyless Day in various Stounds:
Or, louting low, on upstart Fortune fawn,
And sell fair Honour for some paltry Pounds;
Or through the City take your dirty Rounds,
To cheat, and dun, and lye, and Visit pay,
Now flattering base, now giving secret Wounds;
Or proul in Courts of Law for human Prey,
In venal Senate thieve, or rob on broad High-way.

XIV

"No Cocks, with me, to rustic Labour call,
From Village on to Village sounding clear;
To tardy Swain no shrill-voic'd Matrons squall;
No Dogs, no Babes, no Wives, to stun your Ear;

No Hammers thump; no horrid Blacksmith sear,
Ne noisy Tradesman your sweet Slumbers start,
With Sounds that are a Misery to hear :
But all is calm, as would delight the Heart
Of *Sybarite* of old, all Nature, and all Art.

XV

" Here nought but Candour reigns, indulgent Ease,
Good-natur'd Lounging, Sauntering up and down :
They who are pleas'd themselves must always please ;
On Others' Ways they never squint a Frown,
Nor heed what haps in Hamlet or in Town.
Thus, from the Source of tender Indolence,
With milky Blood the Heart is overflown,
Is sooth'd and sweeten'd by the social Sense ;
For Interest, Envy, Pride, and Strife are banish'd hence.

XVI

" What, what, is Virtue, but Repose of Mind ?
A pure ethereal Calm ! that knows no Storm ;
Above the Reach of wild Ambition's Wind,
Above those Passions that this World deform,
And torture Man, a proud malignant Worm !
But here, instead, soft Gales of Passion play,
And gently stir the Heart, thereby to form
A quicker Sense of Joy ; as Breezes stray
Across th' enliven'd Skies, and make them still more gay.

XVII

" The Best of Men have ever lov'd Repose :
They hate to mingle in the filthy Fray ;
Where the Soul sowrs, and gradual Rancour grows,
Imbitter'd more from peevish Day to Day.
Even Those whom Fame has lent her fairest Ray,
The most renown'd of worthy Wights of Yore,
From a base World at last have stolen away :
So *Scipio*, to the soft, *Cumæan* Shore
Retiring, tasted Joy he never knew before.

XVIII

"But if a little Exercise you chuse,
Some Zest for Ease, 'tis not forbidden here.
Amid the Groves you may indulge the Muse,
Or tend the Blooms, and deck the vernal Year;
Or softly stealing, with your watry Gear,
Along the Brooks, the crimson-spotted Fry
You may delude : The whilst, amus'd, you hear
Now the hoarse Stream, and now the Zephir's Sigh,
Attuned to the Birds, and woodland Melody.

XIX

"O grievous Folly! to heap up Estate,
Losing the Days you see beneath the Sun ;
When, sudden, comes blind unrelenting Fate,
And gives th' untasted Portion you have won
With ruthless Toil, and many a Wretch undone,
To Those who mock you gone to *Pluto's* reign,
There with sad Ghosts to pine, and Shadows dun :
But sure it is of Vanities most vain,
To toil for what you here untoiling may obtain."

XX

He ceas'd. But still their trembling Ears retain'd
The deep Vibrations of his witching Song ;
That, by a Kind of Magic Power, constrain'd
To enter in, pell mell, the listening Throng.
Heaps pour'd on Heaps, and yet they slip'd along,
In silent Ease : as when beneath the Beam
Of Summer-Moons, the distant Woods among,
Or by some Flood all silver'd with the Gleam,
The soft-embodied Fays through airy Portal stream. . .

XXIV

Wak'd by the Croud, slow from his Bench arose
A comely full-spred Porter, swoln with Sleep :
His calm, broad, throughtless Aspect breath'd Repose ;

And in sweet Torpor he was plunged deep,
Ne could himself from ceaseless Yawning keep;
While o'er his Eyes the drowsy Liquor ran,
Through which his half-wak'd Soul would faintly peep.
Then taking his black Staff he call'd his Man,
And rous'd himself as much as rouse himself he can.

XXV

The Lad leap'd lightly at his Master's Call.
He was, to weet, a little roguish Page,
Save Sleep and Play who minded nought at all,
Like most the untaught Striplings of his Age.
This Boy he kept each Band to disengage,
Garters and Buckles, Task for him unfit,
But ill-becoming his grave Personage,
And which his portly Paunch would not permit,
So this same limber Page to All performed It.

XXVI

Mean time the Master-Porter wide display'd
Great Store of Caps, of Slippers, and of Gowns;
Wherewith he Those who enter'd in, array'd;
Loose, as the Breeze that plays along the Downs,
And waves the Summer-Woods when Evening frowns.
O fair Undress, best Dress! it checks no Vein,
But ever flowing Limb in Pleasure drowns,
And heightens Ease with Grace. This done, right fain,
Sir Porter sat him down, and turn'd to Sleep again.

XXVII

Thus easy-rob'd, they to the Fountain sped,
That in the Middle of the Court up-threw
A Stream, high-spouting from its liquid Bed,
And falling back again in drizzly Dew:

There Each deep Draughts, as deep he thirsted, drew.
It was a Fountain of *Nepenthe* rare :
Whence, as Dan *Homer* sings, huge Pleasaunce grew,
And sweet Oblivion of vile earthly Care ;
Fair gladsome waking Thoughts, and joyous Dreams more fair.

XXVIII

This Rite perform'd, All inly pleas'd and still,
Withouten Tromp, was Proclamation made.
" Ye Sons of *Indolence*, do what you will ;
And wander where you list, through Hall or Glade :
Be no Man's Pleasure for another's staid ;
Let Each as likes him best his Hours employ,
And curs'd be he who minds his Neighbour's Trade !
Here dwells kind Ease and unreproving Joy :
He little merits Bliss who Others can annoy."

XXIX

Strait of these endless Numbers, swarming round,
As thick as idle Motes in sunny Ray,
Not one eftsoons in View was to be found,
But every Man stroll'd off his own glad Way.
Wide o'er this ample Court's blank Area,
With all the Lodges that thereto pertain'd,
No living Creature could be seen to stray ;
While Solitude, and perfect Silence reign'd :
So that to think you dreamt you almost was constrain'd.

XXX

As when a Shepherd of the *Hebrid-Isles*,
Plac'd far amid the melancholy Main,
(Whether it be lone Fancy him beguiles ;
Or that aërial Beings sometimes deign
To stand, embodied, to our Senses plain)
Sees on the naked Hill, or Valley low,
The whilst in Ocean *Phœbus* dips his Wain,
A vast Assembly moving to and fro :
Then all at once in Air dissolves the wondrous Show.

XXXI

Ye Gods of Quiet, and of Sleep profound!
Whose soft Dominion o'er this Castle sways,
And all the widely-silent Places round,
Forgive me, if my trembling Pen displays
What never yet was sung in mortal Lays.
But how shall I attempt such arduous String?
I who have spent my Nights, and nightly Days,
In this Soul-deadening Place, loose-loitering?
Ah! how shall I for this uprear my moulted Wing?

XXXII

Come on, my Muse, nor stoop to low Despair,
Thou Imp of *Jove*, touch'd by celestial Fire!
Thou yet shalt sing of War, and Actions fair,
Which the bold Sons of *Britain* will inspire;
Of ancient Bards thou yet shalt sweep the Lyre;
Thou yet shalt tread in Tragic Pall the Stage,
Paint Love's enchanting Woes, the Heroe's Ire,
The Sage's Calm, the Patriot's noble Rage,
Dashing Corruption down through every worthless Age.

XXXIII

The Doors, that knew no shrill alarming Bell,
Ne cursed Knocker play'd by Villain's Hand,
Self-open'd into Halls, where, who can tell
What Elegance and Grandeur wide expand
The Pride of *Turkey* and of *Persia* Land?
Soft Quilts on Quilts, on Carpets Carpets spread,
And Couches stretch around in seemly Band;
And endless Pillows rise to prop the Head;
So that each spacious Room was one full-swelling Bed;

XXXIV

And every where huge cover'd Tables stood,
With Wines high-flavour'd and rich Viands crown'd;
Whatever sprightly Juice or tasteful Food
On the green Bosom of the Earth are found,

And all old Ocean genders in his Round :
Some Hand unseen These silently display'd,
Even undemanded, by a Sign or Sound ;
You need but wish, and, instantly obey'd,
Fair-rang'd the Dishes rose, and thick the Glasses
    play'd.

XXXV

Here Freedom reign'd, without the least Alloy ;
Nor Gossip's Tale, nor ancient Maiden's Gall,
Nor saintly Spleen durst murmur at our Joy,
And with envenom'd Tongue our Pleasures pall.
For why ? There was but One great Rule for All ;
To wit, That each should work his own Desire,
And eat, drink, study, sleep, as it may fall,
Or melt the Time in Love, or wake the Lyre,
And carol what, unbid, the Muses might inspire.

XXXVI

The Rooms with costly Tapestry were hung,
Where was inwoven many a gentle Tale ;
Such as of old the rural Poets sung,
Or of *Arcadian* or *Sicilian* Vale :
Reclining Lovers, in the lonely Dale,
Pour'd forth at large the sweetly-tortur'd Heart ;
Or, looking tender Passion, swell'd the Gale,
And taught charm'd Echo to resound their Smart ;
While Flocks, Woods, Streams, around, Repose, and
    Peace impart.

XXXVII

Those pleas'd the most, where, by a cunning Hand,
Depeinten was the Patriarchal Age ;
What time Dan *Abraham* left the *Chaldee* Land,
And pastur'd on from verdant Stage to Stage,

Where Fields and Fountains fresh could best engage.
Toil was not then. Of nothing took they Heed,
But with wild Beasts the silvan War to wage,
And o'er vast Plains their Herds and Flocks to feed :
Blest Sons of Nature they ! True Golden Age indeed !

XXXVIII

Sometimes the Pencil, in cool airy Halls,
Bade the gay Bloom of Vernal Landskips rise,
Or Autumn's varied Shades imbrown the Walls :
Now the black Tempest strikes the astonish'd Eyes ;
Now down the Steep the flashing Torrent flies ;
The trembling Sun now plays o'er Ocean blue,
And now rude Mountains frown amid the Skies ;
Whate'er *Lorrain* light-touch'd with softening Hue,
Or savage *Rosa* dash'd, or learned *Poussin* drew.

XXXI.

Each Sound too here to Languishment inclin'd,
Lull'd the weak Bosom, and induced Ease.
Aërial Music in the warbling Wind,
At Distance rising oft, by small Degrees,
Nearer and nearer came, till o'er the Trees
It hung, and breath'd such Soul-dissolving Airs,
As did, alas ! with soft Perdition please :
Entangled deep in its enchanting Snares,
The listening Heart forgot all Duties and all Cares.

XL

A certain Musick, never known before,
Here lull'd the pensive melancholy Mind ;
Full easily obtain'd. Behoves no more,
But sidelong, to the gently-waving Wind,
To lay the well-tun'd Instrument reclin'd ;
From which, with airy flying Fingers light,
Beyond each mortal Touch the most refin'd,
The Gods of Winds drew sounds of deep Delight :
Whence, with just Cause, *The Harp of Æolus* it hight.

XLI

Ah me ! what Hand can touch the Strings so fine ?
Who up the lofty Diapasan roll
Such sweet, such sad, such so.. nn Airs divine,
Then let them down again into the Soul ?
Now rising Love they fan'd ; now pleasing Dole
They breath'd, in tender Musings, through the Heart;
And now a graver sacred Strain they stole,
As when Seraphic Hands an Hymn impart :
Wild warbling Nature all, above the Reach of Art !

XLII

Such the gay Splendor, the luxurious State,
Of *Caliphs* old, who on the *Tygris*' Shore,
In mighty *Bagdat*, populous and great,
Held their bright Court, where was of Ladies store ;
And Verse, Love, Music still the Garland wore :
When Sleep was coy the Bard, in Waiting there,
Cheer'd the lone Midnight with the Muse's Lore ;
Composing Music bade his Dreams be fair,
And Music lent new Gladness to the Morning Air.

XLIII

Near the Pavilions where we slept, still ran
Soft-tinkling Streams, and dashing Waters fell,
And sobbing Breezes sigh'd, and oft began
(So work'd the Wizard) wintry Storms to swell,
As Heaven and Earth they would together mell :
At Doors and Windows, threatening, seem'd to call
The Demons of the Tempest, growling fell,
Yet the least Entrance found they none at all ;
Whence sweeter grew our Sleep, secure in massy Hall.

XLIV

And hither *Morpheus* sent his kindest Dreams,
Raising a World of gayer Tinct and Grace ;
O'er which were shadowy cast Elysian Gleams,
That play'd, in waving Lights, from Place to Place,

And shed a roseate Smile on Nature's Face.
Not *Titian's* Pencil e'er could so array,
So fleece with Clouds the pure Etherial Space;
Ne could it e'er such melting Forms display,
As loose on flowery Beds all languishingly lay.

XLV

No, fair Illusions! artful Phantoms, no!
My Muse will not attempt your Fairy-Land:
She has no Colours that like you can glow;
To catch your vivid Scenes too gross her Hand.
But sure it is, was ne'er a subtler Band
Than these same guileful Angel-seeming Sprights,
Who thus in Dreams, voluptuous, soft, and bland,
Pour'd all th' *Arabian Heav'n* upon our Nights,
And bless'd them oft besides with more refin'd Delights. . . .

XLIX

One great Amusement of our Household was,
In a huge crystal magic Globe to spy,
Still as you turn'd it, all Things that do pass
Upon this Ant-Hill Earth; where constantly
Of idly-busy Men the restless Fry
Run bustling to and fro with foolish Haste,
In search of Pleasures vain that from them fly,
Or which obtain'd the Caitiffs dare not taste:
When nothing is enjoy'd, can there be greater Waste?

L

Of Vanity the Mirror This was call'd.
Here you a Muckworm of the Town might see,
At his dull Desk, amid his Legers stall'd,
Eat up with carking Care and Penurie;
Most like to Carcase parch'd on Gallow-Tree.
A Penny saved is a Penny got:
Firm to this scoundrel Maxim keepeth he,
Ne of its Rigour will he bate a Jot.
Till it has quench'd his Fire, and banished his Pot.

LI

Straight from the Filth of this low Grub, behold !
Comes fluttering forth a gaudy spendthrift Heir,
All glossy gay, enamel'd all with Gold,
The silly Tenant of the Summer-Air.
In Folly lost, of Nothing takes he Care ;
Pimps, Lawyers, Stewards, Harlots, Flatterers vile,
And thieving Tradesmen him among them share :
His Father's Ghost from Limbo-Lake, the while,
Sees This, which more Damnation does upon him pile.

LII

This Globe pourtray'd the Race of learned Men,
Still at their Books, and turning o'er the Page,
Backwards and forwards : oft they snatch the Pen,
As if inspir'd, and in a *Thespian* Rage ;
Then write, and blot, as would your Ruth engage.
Why, Authors, all this Scrawl and Scribbling sore ?
To lose the present, gain the future Age,
Praised to be when you can hear no more,
And much enrich'd with Fame, when useless worldly
Store.

LIII

Then would a splendid City rise to View,
With Carts, and Cars, and Coaches, roaring all :
Wide-pour'd abroad behold the prowling Crew ;
See ! how they dash along from Wall to Wall ;
At every Door, hark ! how they thundering call.
Good Lord ! what can this giddy Rout excite ?
Why ? On each other with fell Tooth to fall ;
A Neighbour's Fortune, Fame, or Peace, to blight,
And make new tiresome Parties for the coming Night.

LIV

The puzzling Sons of Party next appear'd,
In dark Cabals and nightly Juntos met ;
And now they whisper'd close, now shrugging rear'd
Th' important Shoulder ; then, as if to get

New Light, their twinkling Eyes were inward set,
No sooner *Lucifer* recalls Affairs,
Than forth they various rush in mighty Fret;
When lo! push'd up to Power, and crown'd their Cares,
In comes another Set, and kicketh them down Stairs.

LV

But what most shew'd the Vanity of Life,
Was to behold the Nations all on Fire,
In cruel Broils engag'd, and deadly Strife;
Most Christian Kings, inflam'd by black Desire,
With Honourable Ruffians in their Hire,
Cause War to rage, and Blood around to pour:
Of this sad Work when Each begins to tire,
They sit them down just where they were before,
Till for new Scenes of Woe Peace shall their Force restore.

LVI

To number up the Thousands dwelling here,
A useless were, and eke an endless Task:
From Kings, and Those who at the Helm appear,
To Gipsies brown in Summer-Glades who bask.
Yea many a Man perdie I could unmask,
Whose Desk and Table make a solemn Show,
With Tape-ty'd Trash, and Suits of Fools that ask
For Place or Pension, laid in decent Row;
But These I passen by, with nameless Numbers moe. . . .

[1] LXVIII

A Bard here dwelt, more fat than Bard beseems;
Who void of Envy, Guile, and Lust of Gain,
On Virtue still, and Nature's pleasing Themes,
Pour'd forth his unpremeditated Strain,

[1] The following Lines of this Stanza were writ by a Friend of the Author.

The World forsaking with a calm Disdain :
Here laugh'd he careless in his easy Seat,
Here quaff'd encircled with the joyous Train ;
Oft moralizing sage ; his ditty sweet
He loathed much to write, ne cared to repeat. . . .

LXXI

Here languid Beauty kept her pale-fac'd Court :
Bevies of dainty Dames, of high Degree,
From every Quarter hither made Resort ;
Where, from gross mortal Care and Business free,
They lay, pour'd out in Ease and Luxury.
Or should they a vain Shew of Work assume,
Alas ! and well-a-day ! what can it be ?
To knot, to twist, to range the vernal Bloom ;
But far is cast the Distaff, Spinning-Wheel, and Loom.

LXXII

Their only Labour was to kill the Time ;
And Labour dire it is, and weary Woe.
They sit, they loll, turn o'er some idle Rhyme ;
Then, rising sudden, to the Glass they go,
Or saunter forth, with tottering Step and slow :
This soon too rude an Exercise they find ;
Strait on the Couch their Limbs again they throw,
Where Hours on Hours they sighing lie reclin'd,
And court the vapoury God soft-breathing in the Wind.

JOHN DYER (1700–1757)

GRONGAR HILL

SILENT *Nymph*, with curious Eye !
Who, the purple Evening, lie
On the Mountain's lonely Van,
Beyond the Noise of busy Man,
Painting fair the form of Things,

While the yellow Linnet sings ;
Or the tuneful Nightingale
Charms the Forest with her Tale ;
Come with all thy various Hues,
Come, and aid thy Sister Muse ;
Now while *Phœbus* riding high
Gives Lustre to the Land and Sky !
Grongar Hill invites my Song,
Draw the Landscape bright and strong ;
Grongar, in whose Mossy cells,
Sweetly-musing Quiet dwells :
Grongar, in whose silent Shade,
For the modest Muses made,
So oft I have, the Even still,
At the Fountain of a Rill,
Sat upon a flowery Bed,
With my Hand beneath my Head ;
While stray'd my Eyes o'er *Towy's* flood,
Over Mead, and over Wood,
From House to House, from Hill to Hill,
Till Contemplation had her fill.
  About his chequer'd Sides I wind,
And leave his Brooks and Meads behind,
And Groves, and Grottoes where I lay,
And Vistoes shooting Beams of Day :
Wider and wider spreads the Vale ;
As Circles on a smooth Canal :
The Mountains round, unhappy Fate,
Sooner of later, of all Height !
Withdraw their Summits from the Skies,
And lessen as the others rise :
Still the Prospect wider spreads,
Adds a thousand Woods and Meads,
Still it widens, widens still,
And sinks the newly-risen Hill,
  Now, I gain the Mountain's Brow,
What a Landscape lies below !
No Clouds, no Vapours intervene,
But the gay, the open Scene

Does the Face of Nature show,
In all the Hues of Heaven's Bow!
And, swelling to embrace the Light,
Spreads around beyond the Sight.
 Old Castles on the Cliffs arise,
Proudly tow'ring in the Skies!
Rushing from the Woods, the Spires
Seem from hence ascending Fires!
Half his beams *Apollo* sheds,
On the yellow Mountain-Heads!
Gilds the Fleeces of the Flocks;
And glitters on the broken Rocks!
 Below me Trees unnumber'd rise,
Beautiful in various Dyes:
The gloomy Pine, the Poplar blue,
The yellow Beech, the sable Yew,
The slender Fir, that taper grows,
The sturdy Oak with broad-spread Boughs;
And beyond the purple Grove,
Haunt of *Phillis*, Queen of Love!
Gaudy as the op'ning Dawn,
Lies a long and level Lawn.
On which a dark Hill, steep and high,
Holds and charms the wand'ring Eye!
Deep are his Feet in *Towy's* Flood,
His Sides are cloth'd with waving Wood,
And ancient towers crown his brow,
That cast an awful Look below;
Whose ragged Walls the Ivy creeps,
And with her Arms from falling keeps;
So both a Safety from the Wind
On mutual dependance find.
 'Tis now the Raven's bleak Abode;
'Tis now th' Apartment of the Toad;
And there the Fox securely feeds;
And there the pois'nous Adder breeds,
Conceal'd in Ruins, Moss, and Weeds:
While, ever and anon, there falls,
Huge heaps of hoary moulder'd Walls.

Yet Time has seen, that lifts the low,
And level lays the lofty Brow,
Has seen this broken Pile complete,
Big with the Vanity of State;
But transient is the Smile of Fate!
A little Rule, a little Sway,
A Sun-beam in a Winter's day
Is all the Proud and Mighty have,
Between the Cradle and the Grave.
  And see the Rivers how they run,
Through Woods and Meads, in Shade and Sun,
Sometimes swift, and sometimes slow,
Wave succeeding Wave they go.
A various Journey to the Deep,
Like human Life to endless Sleep!
Thus is Nature's Vesture wrought,
To instruct our wand'ring Thought;
Thus she dresses green and gay,
To disperse our Cares away.
  Ever charming, ever new,
When will the Landscape tire the View!
The Fountain's Fall, the River's Flow,
The woody Valleys, warm and low:
The windy Summit, wild and high,
Roughly rushing on the Sky!
The pleasant Seat, the ruin'd Tow'r,
The naked Rock, the shady Bow'r;
The Town and Village, Dome and Farm,
Each give each a double Charm,
As Pearls upon an *Æthiop's* Arm.
  See on the Mountain's southern side,
Where the Prospect opens wide,
Where the Ev'ning gilds the Tide;
How close and small the Hedges lie!
What streaks of Meadows cross the Eye!
A Step methinks may pass the Stream,
So little distant Dangers seem;
So we mistake the Future's face,
Ey'd thro' Hope's deluding Glass:

As yon Summits soft and fair,
Clad in Colours of the Air,
Which to those who journey near,
Barren, and brown, and rough appear;
Still we tread tir'd the same coarse Way;
The Present's still a cloudy Day.
  O may I with myself agree,
And never covet what I see:
Content me with an humble Shade,
My Passions tam'd, my Wishes laid;
For while our Wishes wildly roll.
We banish Quiet from the Soul:
'Tis thus the Busy beat the Air;
And Misers gather Wealth and Care.
  Now, ev'n now, my Joy runs high,
As on the Mountain-turf I lie;
While the wanton *Zephir* sings,
And in the Vale perfumes his Wings;
While the Waters murmur deep;
While the Shepherd charms his Sheep;
While the Birds unbounded fly,
And with Music fill the Sky,
Now, ev'n now, my Joy runs high.
  Be full, ye Courts; be great who will;
Search for Peace with all your Skill:
Open wide the lofty Door,
Seek her on the marble Floor:
In vain ye search, she is not there;
In vain ye search the Domes of Care!
Grass and Flowers Quiet treads,
On the Meads, and Mountain-heads,
Along with Pleasure, close ally'd,
Ever by each other's Side,
And often, by the murm'ring Rill,
Hears the Thrush, while all is still,
Within the Groves of *Grongar Hill*.

TO HIS SON

TEMPERANCE, exercise, and air,
Make thee strong and debonair;
Quiet, competence, and health,
Furnish thee with real wealth;
Truth, humility, and love,
Lead thee to the bliss above.
More at best, is but a bubble,
More is often toil and trouble.

PHILIP DODDRIDGE (1702–1751)

GOD THE EVERLASTING LIGHT OF THE SAINTS ABOVE

YE golden Lamps of Heav'n, farewell,
　With all your feeble Light:
Farewell, thou ever-changing Moon,
　Pale Empress of the Night.

And thou refulgent Orb of Day
　In brighter Flames array'd,
My Soul, that springs beyond thy Sphere,
　No more demands thine Aid.

Ye Stars are but the shining Dust
　Of my divine Abode,
The Pavement of those heav'nly Courts,
　Where I shall reign with God.

The Father of eternal Light
　Shall there his Beams display;
Nor shall one Moment's Darkness mix
　With that unvaried Day.

No more the Drops of piercing Grief
　Shall swell into mine Eyes;
Nor the Meridian Sun decline
　Amidst those brighter Skies.

> There all the Millions of his Saints
> Shall in one Song unite,
> And Each the Bliss of all shall view
> With infinite Delight.

ISAAC HAWKINS BROWNE (1705-1760)
A PIPE OF TOBACCO
IN IMITATION OF SIX SEVERAL AUTHORS
IMITATION V [POPE]

> *Vanescit* Solis *ad ortus*
> *Fumus.*
>   LUCAN.

BLEST Leaf! whose aromatic Gales dispense
To Templars Modesty, to Parsons sense:
So raptur'd Priests, at fam'd *Dodona's* Shrine
Drank Inspiration from the Steam divine.
Poison that cures, a Vapour that affords
Content, more solid than the Smile of Lords:
Rest to the Weary, to the Hungry Food,
The last kind Refuge of the Wise and Good:
Inspir'd by Thee, dull Cits adjust the Scale
Of *Europe's* Peace, when other statesmen fail.
By Thee protected, and thy Sister, Beer,
Poets rejoice, nor think the Bailiff near.
Nor less, the Critic owns thy genial Aid,
While supperless he plies the piddling Trade.
What tho' to Love and soft Delights a Foe,
By Ladies hated, hated by the Beau,
Yet social Freedom, long to Courts unknown,
Fair Health, fair Truth, and Virtue are thy own.
Come to thy Poet, come with healing Wings,
And let me taste Thee unexcis'd by Kings.

CHARLES WESLEY (1707–1788)
HYMN FOR CHRISTMAS-DAY

HARK how all the Welkin rings
" Glory to the King of Kings,
Peace on Earth, and Mercy mild,
God and Sinners reconcil'd ! "

Joyful all ye Nations rise,
Join the Triumph of the Skies,
Universal Nature say
" Christ the Lord is born To-day ! "

Christ, by highest Heav'n ador'd,
Christ, the everlasting Lord,
Late in Time behold Him come,
Offspring of a Virgin's Womb.

Veil'd in Flesh, the Godhead see,
Hail, th' Incarnate Deity !
Pleas'd as Man with Men t' appear
Jesus, our *Immanuel* here.

Hail, the heav'nly Prince of Peace !
Hail the Sun of Righteousness !
Light and Life to all He brings,
Ris'n with Healing in his Wings.

Mild He lays his Glory by,
Born—that Man no more may die,
Born—to raise the Sons of Earth,
Born—to give them second Birth.

Come, Desire of Nations, come,
Fix in us thy humble Home,
Rise, the Woman's conqu'ring Seed,
Bruise in us the Serpent's Head.

Now display thy saving Power,
Ruin'd Nature now restore,
Now in mystic Union join
Thine to ours, and ours to Thine.

Adam's Likeness, Lord, efface,
Stamp thy Image in its Place,
Second *Adam* from above,
Reinstate us in thy Love.

Let us Thee, tho' lost, regain
Thee, the Life, the inner Man;
O! to All Thyself impart,
Form'd in each believing Heart

★

JESUS, Lord, in Pity hear us,
　　O Return,
　　While we mourn,
By thy Spirit cheer us.

Swallow'd up in Sin and Sadness,
　　O relieve,
　　Us that grieve
Turn our Grief to Gladness.

Send the Comforter to raise us,
　　Let us see
　　God in Thee
Merciful and gracious.

Him the Purchase of thy Passion
　　O impart,
　　Cleanse our Heart
By his Inspiration.

By the Earnest of thy Spirit
　　Let us know
　　Heaven below,
Heaven above inherit.

    Perfect when we walk before thee
        Fill'd with Love,
        Then remove
    To our Thrones of Glory.

★

COME, O Thou traveller unknown,
    Whom still I hold, but cannot see,
My company before is gone,
    And I am left alone with Thee ;
With Thee all night I mean to stay,
And wrestle till the break of day.

I need not tell Thee who I am,
    My misery or sin declare ;
Thyself hast called me by my name ;
    Look on Thy hands, and read it there !
But who, I ask Thee, who art Thou ?
Tell me Thy Name, and tell me now.

In vain Thou strugglest to get free,
    I never will unloose my hold ;
Art Thou the Man who died for me ?
    The secret of Thy love untold.
Wrestling, I will not let Thee go,
Till I Thy name, Thy nature know.

Wilt Thou not yet to me reveal
    Thy new, unutterable Name ?
Tell me, I still beseech Thee, tell :
    To know it now, resolved I am ;
Wrestling, I will not let Thee go,
Till I Thy Name, Thy Nature know. . . .

Yield to me now, for I am weak,
    But confident in self-despair ;
Speak to my heart, in blessings speak,
    Be conquered by my instant prayer !
Speak, or Thou never hence shall move,
And tell me, if Thy Name be Love ?

'Tis Love! 'Tis Love! Thou diedst for me!
　I hear Thy whisper in my heart!
The morning breaks, the shadows flee!
　Pure universal Love Thou art!
To me, to all, Thy bowels move;
Thy nature and Thy Name is Love!

My prayer hath power with God; the grace
　Unspeakable I now receive;
Through faith I see Thee face to face, and live:
　I see Thee face to face, and live:
In vain I have not wept and strove;
Thy nature and Thy Name is Love.

I know Thee, Saviour, who Thou art;
　Jesus, the feeble sinner's Friend!
Nor wilt Thou with the night depart,
　But stay, and love me to the end!
Thy mercies never shall remove,
Thy nature and Thy Name is Love!

The Sun of Righteousness on me
　Hath rose, with healing in his wings;
Withered my nature's strength, from Thee
　My soul its life and succour brings;
My help is all laid up above;
Thy nature and Thy Name is Love.

★

Love Divine, all Loves excelling,
　Joy of Heav'n to Earth come down,
Fix in us thy humble Dwelling,
　All thy faithful Mercies crown;

Jesu, Thou art all Compassion,
　Pure unbounded Love Thou art,
Visit us with thy Salvation,
　Enter every trembling Heart.

Breathe, O breathe thy loving Spirit
  Into every troubled Breast;
Let us all in Thee inherit,
  Let us find that Second Rest:

Take away the *Power* of sinning,
  Alpha and Omega be,
End of Faith as its Beginning,
  Set our Hearts at Liberty.

Come, Almighty to deliver,
  Let us all thy Grace receive,
Suddenly return, and never,
  Never more thy Temples leave.

Thee we would be always blessing,
  Serve thee as thy Hosts above,
Pray, and praise Thee without ceasing,
  Glory in thy perfect Love.

Finish then thy New Creation,
  Pure and sinless let us be,
Let us see thy great Salvation,
  Perfectly restored in Thee;

Chang'd from Glory into Glory,
  Till in Heav'n we take our Place,
Till we cast our Crowns before Thee,
  Lost in Wonder, Love, and Praise!

GEORGE LYTTLETON, LORD LYTTLETON
(1709–1773)
SONG

WHEN *Delia* on the plain appears
Awed by a thousand tender fears,
I would approach, but dare not move;
Tell me, my Heart, if this be Love?

Whene'er she speaks, my ravish'd ear
No other voice but her's can hear,
No other wit but her's approve;
Tell me, my Heart, if this be Love?

If she some other youth commend,
Though I was once his fondest friend,
His instant enemy I prove;
Tell me, my Heart, if this be Love?

When she is absent, I no more
Delight in all that pleas'd before,
The clearest spring, or shadiest grove;
Tell me, my Heart, if this be Love?

When fond of pow'r, or beauty vain,
Her nets she spread for ev'ry swain,
I strove to hate, but vainly strove;
Tell me, my Heart, if this be Love?

SAMUEL JOHNSON (1709–1784)

From THE VANITY OF HUMAN WISHES

In full-blown dignity, see Wolsey stand,
Law in his voice, and fortune in his hand:
To him the church, the realm, their pow'rs consign,
Thro' him the rays of regal bounty shine,
Turn'd by his nod the stream of honour flows,
His smile alone security bestows.
Still to new heights his restless wishes tow'r,
Claim leads to claim, and pow'r advances pow'r:
Till conquest unresisted ceas'd to please,
And rights submitted left him none to seize.
At length his sov'reign frowns—the train of state
Mark the keen glance, and watch the sign to hate.
Where'er he turns, he meets a stranger's eye,
His suppliants scorn him and his followers fly;
Now drops at once the pride of awful state,
The golden canopy, the glitt'ring plate,

The regal palace, the luxurious board,
The liv'ried army, and the menial lord.
With age, with cares, with maladies oppress'd,
He seeks the refuge of monastic rest;
Grief aids disease, remember'd folly stings,
And his last sighs reproach the faith of kings.
 Speak thou whose thoughts at humble peace repine,
Shall Wolsey's wealth, with Wolsey's end, be thine?
Or liv'st thou now, with safer pride content,
The wisest justice on the banks of Trent?
For why did Wolsey, near the steeps of fate,
On weak foundations raise th' enormous weight?
Why, but to sink beneath misfortune's blow,
With louder ruin to the gulfs below?
 What gave great Villiers to th' assassin's knife,
And fix'd disease on Harley's closing life?
What murder'd Wentworth, and what exil'd Hyde,
By kings protected, and to kings ally'd?
What but their wish indulg'd in courts to shine,
And pow'r too great to keep or to resign?
 When first the college rolls receive his name,
The young enthusiast quits his ease of fame;
Thro' all his veins the fever of renown
Burns from the strong contagion of the gown:
O'er Bodley's dome his future labours spread,
And Bacon's mansion trembles o'er his head.
Are these thy views? Proceed, illustrious youth,
And Virtue guard thee to the throne of Truth!
Yet should thy soul indulge the gen'rous heat
Till captive Science yields her last retreat;
Should Reason guide thee with her brightest ray,
And pour on misty doubt resistless day;
Should no false kindness lure to loose delight,
Nor praise relax, nor difficulty fright;
Should tempting Novelty thy cell refrain,
And Sloth effuse her opiate fumes in vain;
Should Beauty blunt on fops her fatal dart,
Nor claim the triumph of a letter'd heart;

Should no disease thy torpid veins invade,
Nor Melancholy's phantoms haunt thy shade;
Yet hope not life from grief or danger free,
Nor think the doom of man revers'd for thee.
Deign on the passing world to turn thine eyes,
And pause awhile from letters to be wise;
There mark what ills the scholar's life assail,
Toil, envy, want, the patron, and the jail.
See nations, slowly wise and meanly just,
To buried merit raise the tardy bust.
If dreams yet flatter, once again attend,
Hear Lydiat's life, and Galileo's end.
  Nor deem, when Learning her last prize bestows,
The glitt'ring eminence exempt from foes;
See, when the vulgar 'scape, despis'd or aw'd,
Rebellion's vengeful talons seize on Laud.
From meaner minds tho' smaller fines content,
The plunder'd palace, or sequester'd rent,
Mark'd out by dang'rous parts, he meets the shock,
And fatal learning leads him to the block:
Around his tomb let Art and Genius weep,
But hear his death, ye blockheads, hear and sleep.
  The festal blazes, the triumphal show,
The ravish'd standard, and the captive foe,
The senate's thanks, the gazette's pompous tale,
With force resistless o'er the brave prevail.
Such bribes the rapid Greek o'er Asia whirl'd,
For such the steady Romans shook the world;
For such in distant lands the Britons shine,
And stain with blood the Danube or the Rhine;
This pow'r has praise, that virtue scarce can warm
Till fame supplies the universal charm.
Yet reason frowns on war's unequal game,
Where wasted nations raise a single name;
And mortgag'd states their grandsires' wreaths regret,
From age to age in everlasting debt;
Wreaths which at last the dear-bought right convey
To rust on medals, or on stones decay.

On what foundation stands the warrior's pride,
How just his hopes, let Swedish Charles decide.
A frame of adamant, a soul of fire,
No dangers fright him, and no labours tire;
O'er love, o'er fear, extends his wide domain,
Unconquer'd lord of pleasure and of pain;
No joys to him pacific sceptres yield,
War sounds the trump, he rushes to the field.
Behold surrounding kings their pow'rs combine,
And one capitulate, and one resign:
Peace courts his hand, but spreads her charms in vain;
"Think nothing gain'd," he cries, "till nought remain,
On Moscow's walls till Gothic standards fly,
And all be mine beneath the polar sky."
The march begins, in military state,
And nations on his eye suspended wait;
Stern Famine guards the solitary coast,
And Winter barricades the realms of Frost;
He comes, nor want nor cold his course delay!—
Hide, blushing glory, hide Pultowa's day:
The vanquish'd hero leaves his broken bands,
And shows his miseries in distant lands;
Condemn'd a needy supplicant to wait,
While ladies interpose, and slaves debate.
But did not Chance at length her error mend?
Did no subverted empire mark his end?
Did rival monarchs give the fatal wound?
Or hostile millions press him to the ground?
His fall was destin'd to a barren strand,
A petty fortress, and a dubious hand;
He left the name at which the world grew pale,
To point a moral, or adorn a tale. . . .
 Where then shall hope and fear their objects find?
Must dull suspense corrupt the stagnant mind?
Must helpless man, in ignorance sedate,
Roll darkling down the torrent of his fate?
Must no dislike alarm, no wishes rise,
No cries invoke the mercies of the skies?

Inquirer, cease : petitions yet remain,
Which Heav'n may hear : nor deem religion vain.
Still raise for good the supplicating voice,
But leave to Heav'n the measure and the choice.
Safe in his pow'r, whose eyes discern afar
The secret ambush of a specious pray'r,
Implore his aid, in his decisions rest,
Secure, what'er he gives, he gives the best.
Yet when the sense of sacred presence fires,
And strong devotion to the skies aspires,
Pour forth thy fervours for a healthful mind,
Obedient passions, and will resign'd ;
For love, which scarce collective man can fill ;
For patience, sov'reign o'er transmuted ill ;
For faith, that, panting for a happier seat,
Counts death kind Nature's signal of retreat.
These goods for man the laws of Heav'n ordain,
These goods he grants, who grants the pow'r to gain ;
With these celestial Wisdom calms the mind,
And makes the happiness she does not find.

[LINES ON THE DEATH OF MR. LEVETT]

CONDEMN'D to Hope's delusive mine,
   As on we toil from day to day,
By sudden blast or slow decline,
   Our social comforts drop away.

Well try'd through many a varying year,
   See *Levett* to the grave descend ;
Officious, innocent, sincere,
   Of ev'ry friendless name the friend.

Yet still he fills Affection's eye,
   Obscurely wise, and coarsely kind,
Nor, letter'd arrogance, deny
   Thy praise to merit unrefin'd.

When fainting Nature call'd for aid,
  And hov'ring Death prepar'd the blow,
His vigorous remedy display'd
  The pow'r of art without the show.

In Misery's darkest caverns known,
  His ready help was ever nigh,
Where hopeless Anguish pours his groan,
  And lonely want retir'd to die.

No summons mock'd by chill delay,
  No petty gains disdain'd by pride;
The modest wants of ev'ry day
  The toil of ev'ry day supply'd.

His virtues walk'd their narrow round,
  Nor made a pause, nor left a void;
And sure th' Eternal Master found
  His single talent well employ'd.

The busy day, the peaceful night,
  Unfelt, uncounted, glided by;
His frame was firm, his powers were bright,
  Though now his eightieth year was nigh.

Then, with no throbs of fiery pain,
  No cold gradations of decay,
Death broke at once the vital chain,
  And freed his soul the nearest way.

WILLIAM SHENSTONE (1714–1763)

From A PASTORAL BALLAD

IN FOUR PARTS

I. ABSENCE

YE shepherds so cheerful and gay,
  Whose flocks never carelessly roam;
Should *Corydon's* happen to stray,
  Oh, call the poor wanderers home.

Allow me to muse and to sigh,
  Nor talk of the change that ye find ;
None once was so watchful as I :
  —I have left my dear *Phyllis* behind.

Now I know what it is, to have strove
  With the torture of doubt and desire ;
What it is, to admire and to love,
  And to leave her we love and admire.
I priz'd every hour that went by,
  Beyond all that had pleas'd me before ;
But now they are past, and I sigh ;
  And I grieve that I priz'd them no more.

But why do I languish in vain ?
  Why wander thus pensively here ?
Oh ! why did I come from the plain,
  Where I fed on the smiles of my dear ?
They tell me, my favourite maid,
  The pride of that valley, is flown ;
Alas ! where with her I have stray'd
  I could wander with pleasure, alone.

When forc'd the fair nymph to forego,
  With anguish I felt at my heart !
Yet I thought—but it might not be so—
  'Twas with pain that she saw me depart.
She gaz'd as I slowly withdrew ;
  My path I could hardly discern ;
So sweetly she bade me adieu,
  I thought that she bade me return.

The pilgrim that journeys all day
  To visit some far-distant shrine,
If he bear but a relic away,
  Is happy, nor heard to repine.
Thus widely remov'd from the fair,
  Where my vows, my devotion, I owe,
Soft hope is the relic I bear,
  And my solace wherever I go.

IV. Disappointment

Ye shepherds give ear to my lay,
  And take no more heed of my sheep;
They have nothing to do, but to stray;
  I have nothing to do, but to weep.
Yet do not my folly reprove;
  She was fair—and my passion begun;
She smil'd—and I could not but love;
  She is faithless—and I am undone.

Perhaps I was void of all thought;
  Perhaps it was plain to foresee,
That a nymph so complete would be sought
  By a swain more engaging than me.
Ah! love ev'ry hope can inspire:
  It banishes wisdom the while;
And the lip of the nymph we admire
  Seems for ever adorn'd with a smile.

She is faithless, and I am undone;
  Ye that witness the woes I endure,
Let reason instruct you to shun
  What it cannot instruct you to cure.
Beware how you loiter in vain
  Amid nymphs of an higher degree:
It is not for me to explain
  How fair, and how fickle they be.

Alas! from the day that we met,
  What hope of an end to my woes?
When I cannot endure to forget
  The glance that undid my repose.
Yet time may diminish the pain:
  The flower, and the shrub, and the tree,
Which I rear'd for her pleasure in vain,
  In time may have comfort for me.

The sweets of a dew-sprinkled rose,
    The sound of a murmuring stream,
The peace which from solitude flows,
    Henceforth shall be *Corydon's* theme.
High transports are shown to the sight,
    But we are not to find them our own;
Fate never bestow'd such delight,
    As I with my *Phyllis* had known.

O ye woods, spread your branches apace;
    To your deepest recesses I fly;
I would hide with the beasts of the chase;
    I would vanish from every eye.
Yet my reed shall resound through the grove
    With the same sad complaint it begun;
How she smil'd, and I could not but love;
    Was faithless, and I am undone!

SONG XII. 1744

O'ER desert plains, and rushy meres,
    And wither'd heaths I rove;
Where tree, nor spire, nor cot appears,
    I pass to meet my love.

But, though my path were damask'd o'er
    With beauties e'er so fine;
My busy thoughts would fly before,
    To fix alone—on thine.

No fir-crown'd hills could give delight,
    No palace please mine eye;
No pyramid's aërial height,
    Where mouldering monarchs lie.

Unmov'd, should Eastern kings advance;
    Could I the pageant see:
Splendour might catch one scornful glance,
    Not steal one thought from thee.

WRITTEN AT AN INN AT HENLEY

To thee, fair freedom ! I retire
  From flattery, cards, and dice, and din ;
Nor art thou found in mansions higher
  Than the low cot or humble inn.

'Tis here with boundless power I reign ;
  And every health which I begin,
Converts dull port to bright champagne ;
  Such freedom crowns it, at an inn.

I fly from pomp, I fly from plate !
  I fly from falsehood's specious grin !
Freedom I love, and form I hate,
  And choose my lodgings at an inn.

Here, waiter, take my sordid ore,
  Which laqueys else might hope to win ;
It buys, what courts have not in store ;
  It buys me freedom, at an inn.

Who'er has travell'd life's dull round,
  Where'er his stages may have been,
May sigh to think he still has found
  The warmest welcome, at an inn.

THE SCHOOL-MISTRESS

A POEM IN IMITATION OF SPENSER

ADVERTISEMENT

What particulars in Spenser were imagin'd most proper for the author's imitation on *this occasion*, are, his *language*, his *simplicity*, his manner of *description*, and a peculiar *tenderness* of *sentiment*, remarkable throughout his works.

I

AH me ! full sorely is my heart forlorn,
To think how modest worth neglected lies !
While partial Fame doth with her blasts adorn
Such deeds alone, as pride and pomp disguise ;

Deeds of ill sort, and mischievous emprize !
Lend me thy clarion, goddess ! let me try
To sound the praise of merit, ere it dies ;
Such as I oft have chaunced to espy,
Lost in the dreary shades of dull obscurity.

II

In ev'ry village mark'd with little spire,
Embow'r'd in trees, and hardly known to Fame,
There dwells in lowly shed, and mean attire,
A matron old, whom we School-mistress name ;
Who boasts unruly brats with birch to tame :
They grieven sore, in piteous durance pent,
Aw'd by the pow'r of this relentless dame ;
And oft-times, on vagaries idly bent,
For unkempt hair, or task unconn'd, are sorely shent.

III

And all in sight doth rise a birchen tree,
Which Learning near Her little dome did stowe,
Whilom a twig of small regard to see,
Tho' now so wide its waving branches flow ;
And work the simple vassals mickle woe :
For not a wind might curl the leaves that blew,
But their limbs shudder'd, and their pulse beat low ;
And, as thy look'd, they found their horror grew,
And shap'd it into rods, and tingled at the view.

IV

So have I seen (who has not, may conceive),
A lifeless phantom near a garden plac'd :
So doth it wanton birds of peace bereave,
Of sport, of song, of pleasure, of repast ;

They start, they stare, they wheel, they look aghast:
Sad servitude! such comfortless annoy
May no bold Briton's riper age e'er taste!
Ne Superstition clog his dance of joy,
Ne vision empty, vain, his native bliss destroy.

V

Near to this dome is found a patch so green,
On which the tribe their gambols do display:
And at the door impris'ning board is seen,
Lest weakly wights of smaller size should stray;
Eager, perdie, to bask in sunny day!
The noises intermix'd, which thence resound,
Do Learning's little tenement betray:
Where sits the dame, disguis'd in look profound,
And eyes her fairy throng, and turns her wheel around.

VI

Her cap, far whiter than the driven snow,
Emblem right meet of decency does yield:
Her apron dy'd in grain, as blue, I trowe,
As is the Hare-bell that adorns the field;
And in her hand, for sceptre, she does wield
Tway birchen sprays; with anxious Fear entwin'd,
With dark Distrust, and sad Repentance fill'd;
And stedfast Hate, and sharp Affliction join'd,
And Fury uncontroul'd, and Chastisement unkind.

VII

Few but have ken'd, in semblance meet pourtray'd,
The childish faces, of old Eol's train;
Libs, Notus, Auster : These in frowns array'd,
How then would fare or earth, or sky, or main,

Were the stern god to give his slaves the rein?
And were not she rebellious breasts to quell,
And were not she her statutes to maintain,
The cott no more, I ween, were deem'd the cell,
Where comely peace of mind, and decent order dwell.

VIII

A russet stole was o'er her shoulders thrown;
A russet kirtle fenc'd the nipping air;
'Twas simple russet, but it was her own;
'Twas her own country bred the flock so fair;
'Twas her own labour did the fleece prepare;
And, sooth to say, her pupils, rang'd around,
Through pious awe, did term it passing rare;
For they in gaping wonderment abound,
And think, no doubt, she been the greatest wight on ground.

IX

Albeit ne flatt'ry did corrupt her truth,
Ne pompous title did debauch her ear;
Goody, good-woman, gossip, n'aunt, forsooth,
Or dame, the sole Additions she did hear;
Yet these she challeng'd, these she held right dear:
Ne would esteem him act as mought behove,
Who should not honour'd eld with these revere:
For never title yet so mean could prove,
But there was eke a Mind which did that title love.

X

One ancient hen she took delight to feed,
The plodding pattern of the busy dame;
Which, ever and anon, impell'd by need,
Into her School, begirt with chickens, came;

Such favour did her past deportment claim :
And, if Neglect had lavish'd on the ground
Fragment of bread, she would collect the same ;
For well she knew, and quaintly could expound,
What sin it were to waste the smallest crumb she
 found.

XI

Herbs too, she knew, and well of each could speak
That in her garden sip'd the silv'ry dew ;
Where no vain flow'r disclos'd a gaudy streak ;
But herbs for use, and physick, not a few,
Of grey renown, within those borders grew :
The tufted Basil, pun-provoking Tyme,
Fresh Baum, and Marygold of chearful hue ;
The lowly Gill, that never dares to climb ;
And more I fain would sing, disdaining here to
 rhime.

XII

Yet Euphrasy may not be left unsung,
That gives dim eyes to wander leagues around ;
And pungent Radish, biting infant's tongue ;
And Plantain ribb'd, that heals the reaper's wound ;
And Marj'ram sweet, in shepherd's posie found ;
And Lavender, whose pikes of azure bloom
Shall be, ere-while, in arid bundles bound,
To lurk amidst the labours of her loom,
And crown her kerchiefs clean, with mickle rare
 perfume.

XIII

And here trim Rosmarine, that whilom crown'd
The daintiest garden of the proudest peer ;
Ere, driven from its envy'd site, it found
A sacred shelter for its branches here ;

Where edg'd with gold its glitt'ring skirts appear.
O wassel days! O customs meet and well!
Ere this was banish'd from its lofty sphere;
Simplicity then sought this humble cell,
Nor ever would She more with thane or lordling dwell.

XIV

Here oft the dame, on Sabbath's decent eve,
Hymned such psalms as Sternhold forth did mete,
If winter 'twere, she to her hearth did cleave;
But in her garden found a summer seat:
Sweet melody! to hear her then repeat
How Israel's sons, beneath a foreign king,
While taunting foe-men did a song intreat,
All, for the Nonce, untuning ev'ry string,
Uphung their useless lyres—small heart had they to sing.

XV

For she was just, and friend to virtuous lore,
And pass'd much time in truly virtuous deed;
And, in those Elfin's ears, would oft deplore,
The times, when Truth by Popish rage did bleed;
And tortious death was true devotion's meed;
And simple faith in iron chains did mourn,
That nould on wooden image place her creed;
And lawny saints in smould'ring flames did burn:
Ah! dearest Lord, forfend thilk days should e'er return!

XVI

In elbow-chair, like that of Scottish stem
By the sharp tooth of cank'ring eld defac'd,
In which, when he receives his diadem,
Our sovereign prince and liefest liege is plac'd,

The matron sate ; and some with rank she grac'd,
(The source of children's and of courtier's pride !)
Redress'd affronts, for vile affronts there pass'd ;
And warn'd them not the fretful to deride,
But love each other dear, whatever them betide.

XVII

Right well she knew each temper to descry ;
To thwart the proud, and the submiss to raise ;
Some with vile copper prize exalt on high,
And some entice with pittance small of praise ;
And other some with baleful sprig she 'frays :
Ev'n absent, she the reins of pow'r doth hold,
While with quaint arts the giddy crowd she sways ;
Forewarn'd, if little bird their pranks behold,
'Twill whisper in her ear, and all the scene unfold.

XVIII

Lo now with state she utters the command !
Eftsoons the urchins to their tasks repair :
Their books of stature small they take in hand,
Which with pellucid horn secured are,
To save from finger wet the letters fair ;
The work so gay, that on their backs is seen,
St. George's high atchievements does declare,
On which thilk wight that has y-gazing been,
Kens the forthcoming rod, unpleasing sight, I ween ! . . .

XXVIII

Yet nurs'd with skill what dazling fruits appear !
Ev'n now sagacious Foresight points to show
A little bench of heedless bishops here,
And there a chancellour in embryo,

Or 'bard sublime, if bard may e'er be so,
As Milton, Shakspeare, names that ne'er shall dye!
Though now he crawl along the ground so low,
Nor weeting how the muse should soar on high,
Wisheth, poor starvling elf! his paper-kite may fly.

XXIX

And this perhaps, who, cens'ring the Design,
Low lays the house which that of cards doth build,
Shall Dennis be! if rigid fates incline,
And many an Epick to his rage shall yield;
And many a poet quit th' Aonian field;
And, sour'd by age, profound he shall appear,
As he who now with 'sdeignfull fury thrill'd
Surveys mine work, and levels many a sneer,
And furls his wrinkly front, and cries "What stuff
  is here!"

XXX

But now Dan Phœbus gains the middle skie,
And Liberty unbars their prison-door;
And like a rushing torrent out they fly,
And now the grassy cirque han cover'd o'er
With boist'rous revel-rout and wild uproar;
A thousand ways in wanton rings they run,
Heav'n shield their short-liv'd pastimes, I implore!
For well may freedom, erst so dearly won,
Appear to British elf more gladsome than the sun.

XXXI

Enjoy, poor imps! enjoy your sportive trade;
And chase gay flies and cull the fairest flow'rs,
For when my bones in grass-green sods are laid,
For never may ye taste more careless hours

In knightly castles, or in ladies' bow'rs.
   O vain to seek delight in earthly thing!
   But most in courts where proud ambition tow'rs;
   Deluded wight! who weens fair peace can spring
Beneath the pompous dome of Kesar or of king.

XXXII

   See in each sprite some various bent appear!
   These rudely carol most incondite lay;
   Those, saunt'ring on the green, with jocund leer
   Salute the stranger passing on his way;
   Some builden fragile tenements of clay;
   Some to the standing lake their courses bend,
   With pebbles smooth at Duck and Drake to play;
   Thilk to the huxter's sav'ry cottage tend,
In pastry kings and queens th' allotted mite to spend.

XXXIII

   Here, as each season yields a different store,
   Each season's stores in order ranged been;
   Apples with cabbage-net y-cover'd o'er,
   Galling full sore th' unmoney'd wight, are seen;
   And goose-b'rie clad in liv'ry red or green;
   And here of lovely dye, the Cath'rine-pear,
   Fine pear! as lovely for thy juice, I ween:
   O may no wight e'er penny-less come there,
Lest smit with ardent love he pine with hopeless care!

XXXIV

   See! cherries here, ere cherries yet abound,
   With thread so white in tempting posies ty'd,
   Scatt'ring like blooming maid their glances round,
   With pamper'd look draw little eyes aside;

And must be bought though penury betide;
The plumb all azure and the nut all brown,
And here, each season, do those cakes abide,
Whose honour'd names th' inventive city own,
Rend'ring through Britain's isle Salopia's praises
known.[1]

XXXV

Admir'd Salopia! that with venial pride
Eyes her bright form in Severn's ambient wave;
Fam'd for her loyal cares in perils tried.
Her daughters lovely, and her striplings brave:
Ah! 'midst the rest, may flowers adorn His grave,
Whose art did first these dulcet cates display!
A motive fair to Learning's imps he gave,
Who chearless o'er her darkling region stray;
'Till reason's morn arise, and light them on their
way.

WILLIAM WHITEHEAD (1715-1785)

THE JE NE SCAI QUOI

Yes, I'm in love, I feel it now,
   And *Cælia* has undone me;
And yet I'll swear I can't tell how
   The pleasing plague stole on me.

'Tis not her face that love creates,
   For there no graces revel;
'Tis not her shape, for there the fates
   Have rather been uncivil.

'Tis not her air, for sure in that
   There's nothing more than common;
And all her sense is only chat,
   Like any other woman.

[1] Shrewsbury cakes.

Her voice, her touch might give th' alarm—
'Twas both perhaps, or neither ;
In short, 'twas that provoking charm
Of *Cælia* altogether.

THOMAS GRAY (1716–1771)

SONNET

ON THE DEATH OF RICHARD WEST

In vain to me the smiling Mornings shine,
And redd'ning Phœbus lifts his golden fire :
The birds in vain their amorous descant join ;
Or cheerful fields resume their green attire :
These ears, alas ! for other notes repine,
A different object do these eyes require :
My lonely anguish melts no heart but mine ;
And in my breast the imperfect joys expire.
Yet Morning smiles the busy race to cheer,
And new-born pleasure brings to happier men :
The fields to all their wonted tribute bear :
To warm their little loves the birds complain ;
I fruitless mourn to him, that cannot hear,
And weep the more, because I weep in vain.

ELEGY
WRITTEN IN A COUNTRY CHURCH-YARD

The curfew tolls the knell of parting day,
The lowing herd wind slowly o'er the lea,
The ploughman homeward plods his weary way,
And leaves the world to darkness and to me.

Now fades the glimmering landscape on the sight,
And all the air a solemn stillness holds,
Save where the beetle wheels his droning flight,
And drowsy tinklings lull the distant folds :

Save that from yonder ivy-mantled tower
The moping owl does to the moon complain
Of such as, wandering near her secret bower,
Molest her ancient solitary reign.

Beneath those rugged elms, that yew-tree's shade,
Where heaves the turf in many a mouldering heap,
Each in his narrow cell for ever laid,
The rude Forefathers of the hamlet sleep.

The breezy call of incense-breathing morn,
The swallow twittering from the straw-built shed,
The cock's shrill clarion, or the echoing horn,
No more shall rouse them from their lowly bed.

For them no more the blazing hearth shall burn
Or busy housewife ply her evening care:
No children run to lisp their sire's return,
Or climb his knees the envied kiss to share.

Oft did the harvest to their sickle yield,
Their furrow oft the stubborn glebe has broke;
How jocund did they drive their team afield!
How bowed the woods beneath their sturdy stroke!

Let not Ambition mock their useful toil,
Their homely joys, and destiny obscure;
Nor Grandeur hear with a disdainful smile
The short and simple annals of the Poor.

The boast of heraldry, the pomp of power,
And all that beauty, all that wealth e'er gave,
Await alike th' inevitable hour :—
The paths of glory lead but to the grave.

Nor you, ye Proud, impute to these the fault
If Memory o'er their tomb no trophies raise,
Where through the long-drawn aisle and fretted vault
The pealing anthem swells the note of praise.

Can storied urn or animated bust
Back to its mansion call the fleeting breath ?
Can Honour's voice provoke the silent dust,
Or Flattery soothe the dull cold ear of Death ?

Perhaps in this neglected spot is laid
Some heart once pregnant with celestial fire ;
Hands, that the rod of empire might have swayed.
Or waked to ecstasy the living lyre :

But Knowledge to their eyes her ample page
Rich with the spoils of time, did ne'er unroll ;
Chill Penury repressed their noble rage,
And froze the genial current of the soul.

Full many a gem of purest ray serene
The dark unfathomed caves of ocean bear :
Full many a flower is born to blush unseen,
And waste its sweetness on the desert air.

Some village-Hampden, that with dauntless breast
The little tyrant of his fields withstood,
Some mute inglorious Milton here may rest,
Some Cromwell, guiltless of his country's blood.

Th' applause of list'ning senates to command,
The threats of pain and ruin to despise,
To scatter plenty o'er a smiling land,
And read their history in a nation's eyes,

Their lot forbad : nor circumscribed alone
Their growing virtues, but their crimes confined ;
Forbad to wade through slaughter to a throne,
And shut the gates of mercy on mankind ;

The struggling pangs of conscious truth to hide,
To quench the blushes of ingenuous shame,
Or heap the shrine of Luxury and Pride
With incense kindled at the Muse's flame.

Far from the madding crowd's ignoble strife
Their sober wishes never learned to stray;
Along the cool sequestered vale of life
They kept the noiseless tenour of their way.

Yet e'en these bones from insult to protect
Some frail memorial still erected nigh,
With uncouth rhymes and shapeless sculpture decked,
Implores the passing tribute of a sigh.

Their name, their years, spelt by th' unlettered Muse,
The place of fame and elegy supply:
And many a holy text around she strews
That teach the rustic moralist to die.

For who, to dumb forgetfulness a prey,
This pleasing anxious being e'er resigned,
Left the warm precincts of the cheerful day,
Nor cast one longing lingering look behind?

On some fond breast the parting soul relies,
Some pious drops the closing eye requires;
E'en from the tomb the voice of Nature cries,
E'en in our ashes live their wonted fires.

For thee, who, mindful of th' unhonoured dead,
Dost in these lines their artless tale relate;
If chance, by lonely Contemplation led,
Some kindred spirit shall inquire thy fate,—

Haply some hoary-headed swain may say,
Oft have we seen him at the peep of dawn
Brushing with hasty steps the dews away,
To meet the sun upon the upland lawn;

There at the foot of yonder nodding beech,
That wreathes its old fantastic roots so high,
His listless length at noon-tide would he stretch,
And pore upon the brook that babbles by.

Hard by yon wood, now smiling as in scorn,
Muttering his wayward fancies he would rove;
Now drooping, woeful-wan, like one forlorn,
Or crazed with care, or crossed in hopeless love.

One morn I missed him on the customed hill,
Along the heath, and near his favourite tree;
Another came; nor yet beside the rill,
Nor up the lawn, nor at the wood was he;

The next with dirges due in sad array
Slow through the church-way path we saw him
 borne,—
Approach and read (for thou canst read) the lay
Graved on the stone beneath yon aged thorn.

Here rests his head upon the lap of Earth
A Youth, to Fortune and to Fame unknown;
Fair Science frowned not on his humble birth,
And Melancholy marked him for her own.

Large was his bounty, and his soul sincere;
Heaven did a recompense as largely send:
He gave to Misery all he had, a tear,
He gained from Heaven, 'twas all he wished, a friend.

No farther seek his merits to disclose,
Or draw his frailties from their dread abode,
(There they alike in trembling hope repose,)
The bosom of his Father and his God.

ON A FAVOURITE CAT, DROWNED IN A TUB OF GOLD FISHES

'Twas on a lofty vase's side
Where China's gayest art had dyed
The azure flowers that blow,
Demurest of the tabby kind
The pensive Selima, reclined,
Gazed on the lake below.

Her conscious tail her joy declared :
The fair round face, the snowy beard,
The velvet of her paws,
Her coat that with the tortoise vies,
Her ears of jet, and emerald eyes—
She saw, and purred applause.

Still had she gazed, but 'midst the tide
Two angel forms were seen to glide,
The Genii of the stream :
Their scaly armour's Tyrian hue
Through richest purple, to the view
Betrayed a golden gleam.

The hapless Nymph with wonder saw :
A whisker first, and then a claw
With many an ardent wish
She stretched, in vain, to reach the prize—
What female heart can gold despise ?
What Cat's averse to Fish ?

Presumptuous maid ! with looks intent
Again she stretched, again she bent,
Nor knew the gulf between—
Malignant Fate sat by and smiled—
The slippery verge her feet beguiled ;
She tumbled headlong in !

Eight times emerging from the flood
She mewed to every watery God
Some speedy aid to send :—
No Dolphin came, no Nereid stirred,
Nor cruel Tom nor Susan heard—
A favourite has no friend !

From hence, ye Beauties! undeceived,
Know one false step is ne'er retrieved,
And be with caution bold:
Not all that tempts your wandering eyes
And heedless hearts, is lawful prize,
Nor all that glisters, gold!

THE PROGRESS OF POESY

A PINDARIC ODE

AWAKE, Aeolian lyre, awake,
And give to rapture all thy trembling strings.
From Helicon's harmonious springs
A thousand rills their mazy progress take:
The laughing flowers that round them blow
Drink life and fragrance as they flow.
Now the rich stream of Music winds along
Deep, majestic, smooth, and strong.
Through verdant vales, and Ceres' golden reign;
Now rolling down the steep amain
Headlong, impetuous, see it pour:
The rocks and nodding groves re-bellow to the
    roar. . . .

Woods, that wave o'er Delphi's steep,
Isles, that crown th' Aegean deep,
Fields that cool Ilissus laves,
Or where Maeander's amber waves
In lingering lab'rinths creep,
How do your tuneful echoes languish,
Mute, but to the voice of anguish!
Where each old poetic mountain
    Inspiration breathed around;
Every shade and hallowed fountain
    Murmured deep a solemn sound:
Till the sad Nine, in Greece's evil hour,

Left their Parnassus for the Latian plains.
Alike they scorn the pomp of tyrant Power.
And coward Vice, that revels in her chains.
When Latium had her lofty spirit lost,
They sought, O Albion! next, thy sea-encircled coast.

    Far from the sun and summer-gale
In thy green lap was Nature's Darling laid,
What time, where lucid Avon strayed,
    To him the mighty mother did unveil
Her awful face: the dauntless Child
Stretched forth his little arms, and smiled.
This pencil take (she said), whose colours clear
Richly paint the vernal year:
Thine, too, these golden keys, immortal Boy!
This can unlock the gates of Joy;
Of Horror that, and thrilling Fears,
Or ope the sacred source of sympathetic Tears.

    Nor second He, that rode sublime
Upon the seraph-wings of Ecstasy
The secrets of the Abyss to spy:
    He passed the flaming bounds of Place and Time:
The living Throne, the sapphire-blaze
Where Angels tremble while they gaze,
He saw; but blasted with excess of light,
Closed his eyes in endless night.
Behold where Dryden's less presumptuous car
Wide o'er the fields of Glory bear
Two coursers of ethereal race
With necks in thunder clothed, and long-resounding
    pace.

Hark, his hands the lyre explore!
Bright-eyed Fancy, hovering o'er,
Scatters from her pictured urn
Thoughts that breathe, and words that burn.
But ah! 'tis heard no more——

O ! Lyre divine, what daring Spirit
Wakes thee now ! Tho' he inherit
Nor the pride, nor ample pinion,
   That the Theban Eagle bear,
Sailing with supreme dominion
   Thro' the azure deep of air :
Yet oft before his infant eyes would run
  Such forms as glitter in the Muse's ray
With orient hues, unborrow'd of the sun :
  Yet shall he mount, and keep his distant way
Beyond the limits of a vulgar fate :
Beneath the Good how far—but far above the Great.

FRANCES GREVILLE

PRAYER FOR INDIFFERENCE. 1755

OFT I've implor'd the gods in vain,
   And pray'd till I've been weary :
For once I'll seek my wish to gain
   Of Oberon the fairy.

Sweet airy Being, wanton Spright,
   Who liv'st in woods unseen ;
And oft by Cynthia's silver light
   Trip'st gaily o'er the green ;

If e'er thy pitying heart was mov'd
   As ancient stories tell ;
And for th' Athenian maid who lov'd,
   Thou sought'st a wondrous spell,

O ! deign once more t' exert thy power !
   Haply some herb or tree,
Sovereign as juice from western flower,
   Conceals a balm for me.

I ask no kind return in love,
   No tempting charm to please ;
Far from the heart such gifts remove,
   That sighs for peace and ease !

A.E.P.   F

Nor ease, nor peace, that heart can know,
  That, like the needle true,
Turns at the touch of joy or woe;
  But, turning, trembles too.

Far as distress the soul can wound,
  'Tis pain in each degree:
'Tis bliss but to a certain bound—
  Beyond—is agony.

Then take this treacherous sense of mine,
  Which dooms me still to smart;
Which pleasure can to pain refine;
  To pain new pangs impart.

O! haste to shed the sovereign balm,
  My shatter'd nerves new-string;
And for my guest, serenely calm,
  The nymph Indifference bring! . . .

And what of life remains for me,
  I'll pass in sober ease;
Half-pleas'd, contented will I be,
  Content—but half to please.

DAVID GARRICK (1717–1779)

WARWICKSHIRE

(WRITTEN FOR THE SHAKESPEARE JUBILEE)

Ye Warwickshire lads, and ye lasses,
See what at our Jubilee passes,
Come revel away, rejoice and be glad,
For the lad of all lads, was a Warwickshire lad,
    Warwickshire lad,
      All be glad,
For the lad of all lads, was a Warwickshire lad.

Be proud of the charms of your county,
Where Nature has lavish'd her bounty,
Where much she has giv'n, and some to be spar'd,
For the bard of all bards, was a Warwickshire bard,
    Warwickshire bard,
      Never pair'd,
For the bard of all bards, was a Warwickshire bard.

Each shire has its different pleasures,
Each shire has its different treasures;
But to rare Warwickshire all must submit,
For the wit of all wits, was a Warwickshire wit,
    Warwickshire wit,
      How he writ!
For the wit of all wits, was a Warwickshire wit.

Old Ben, Thomas Otway, John Dryden,
And half a score more we take pride in,
Of famous Will Congreve, we boast too the skill,
But the Will of all Wills, was a Warwickshire Will,
    Warwickshire Will,
      Matchless still,
For the Will of all Wills, was a Warwickshire Will.

Our Shakespeare compar'd is to no man,
Nor Frenchman, nor Grecian, nor Roman,
Their swans are all geese, to the Avon's sweet swan,
And the man of all men, was a Warwickshire man,
    Warwickshire man,
      Avon's swan,
And the man of all men, was a Warwickshire man.

As ven'son is very inviting,
To steal it our bard took delight in,
To make his friends merry he never was lag,
And the wag of all wags, was a Warwickshire wag,
    Warwickshire wag,
      Ever brag,
For the wag of all wags, was a Warwickshire wag.

There never was seen such a creature,
Of all she was worth, he robb'd Nature!
He took all her smiles, and he took all her grief,
And the thief of all thieves, was a Warwickshire thief,
    Warwickshire thief,
    He's the chief,
For the thief of all thieves, was a Warwickshire thief.

WILLIAM WILLIAMS (1717–1791)

"ARGLWYDD ARWAIN TRWY'R ANIALWCH"

GUIDE me, O thou great Jehovah,
Pilgrim thro' this barren land;
I am weak, but thou art mighty,
Hold me with thy pow'rful hand:
Bread of heav'n, bread of heav'n,
Feed me till I want no more.

Open now the crystal fountain,
Whence the healing stream doth flow;
Let the fire and cloudy pillar
Lead me all my journey thro':
Strong deliv'rer, strong deliv'rer,
Be thou still my strength and shield.

When I tread the verge of Jordan,
Bid my anxious fears subside;
Death of deaths, and hell's destruction,
Land me safe on Canaan's side:
Songs of praises, songs of praises
I will ever give to thee.

Musing on my habitation,
Musing on my heav'nly home,
Fills my soul with holy longing:
Come, my Jesus, quickly come;
Vanity is all I see;
Lord, I long to be with thee!

HORACE WALPOLE, EARL OF ORFORD (1717-1797)

COUNTESS *TEMPLE*, APPOINTED *POET LAUREATE* TO THE *KING* OF THE *FAIRIES*

By these presents be it known,
To all who bend before our throne,
Fays and fairies, elves and sprites,
Beauteous dames and gallant knights,
That we, Oberon the grand,
Emperor of Fairy-Land,
King of moonshine, prince of dreams,
Lord of Aganippe's streams,
Baron of the dimpled isles
That lie in pretty maidens' smiles,
Arch-treasurer of all the graces
Dispers'd through fifty lovely faces,
Sovereign of the slipper's order,
With all the rites thereon that border,
Defender of the sylphic faith,
Declare—and thus your monarch saith:

Whereas there is a noble dame,
Whom mortals Countess Temple name,
To whom ourself did erst impart
The choicest secrets of our art,
Taught her to tune th' harmonious line
To our own melody divine,
Taught her the graceful negligence,
Which, scorning art and veiling sense,
Achieves that conquest o'er the heart
Sense seldom gains, and never art:
This lady, 'tis our royal will
Our Laureate's vacant seat should fill;
A chaplet of immortal bays
Shall crown her brow and guard her lays;

Of nectar sack, an acorn cup
Be at her board each year fill'd up;
And as each quarter feast comes round
A silver penny shall be found
Within the compass of her shoe—
And so we bid you all adieu.

Given at our palace of Cowslip-Castle, the shortest night of the year.—OBERON.

SONG

WHAT a rout do you make for a single poor kiss!
I seiz'd it, 'tis true, and I ne'er shall repent it;
May he ne'er enjoy one, who shall think 'twas amiss!
But for me, I thank dear Cytherea, who sent it.

You may pout, and look prettily cross; but I pray,
What business so near to my lips had your cheek?
If you will put temptation so pat in one's way,
Saints, resist if ye can; but for me, I'm too weak.

But come, my sweet Fanny, our quarrel let's end;
Nor will I by force what you gave not, retain:
By allowing the kiss, I'm for ever your friend—
If you say that I stole it, why take it again.

WILLIAM COLLINS (1721–1759)
ODE

WRITTEN IN THE BEGINNING OF THE YEAR 1746

How sleep the Brave, who sink to Rest,
By all their Country's Wishes blest!
When *Spring*, with dewy Fingers cold,
Returns to deck their hallow'd Mould,
She there shall dress a sweeter Sod,
Than *Fancy's* Feet have ever trod.

By Fairy Hands their knell is rung,
By Forms unseen their Dirge is sung;
There *Honour* comes, a Pilgrim grey,
To bless the Turf that wraps their Clay,
And Freedom shall a-while repair,
To dwell a weeping Hermit there!

ODE ON THE DEATH OF THOMSON

IN yonder grave a Druid lies,
   Where slowly winds the stealing wave!
The year's best sweets shall duteous rise
   To deck its Poet's sylvan grave!

In yon deep bed of whisp'ring reeds
   His airy harp shall now be laid,
That he, whose heart in sorrow bleeds,
   May love thro' life the soothing shade.

Then maids and youths shall linger here,
   And while its sounds at distance swell,
Shall sadly seem in Pity's ear
   To hear the Woodland Pilgrim's knell.

Remembrance oft shall haunt the shore
   When Thames in summer wreaths is drest,
And oft suspend the dashing oar
   To bid his gentle spirit rest!

And oft as Ease and Health retire
   To breezy lawn, or forest deep,
The friend shall view yon whitening spire,
   And 'mid the varied landscape weep.

But thou, who own'st that earthy bed,
   Ah! what will every dirge avail?
Or tears, which Love and Pity shed,
   That mourn beneath the gliding sail?

Yet lives there one, whose heedless eye
    Shall scorn thy pale shrine glimm'ring near?
With him, sweet bard, may Fancy die,
    And Joy desert the blooming year.

But thou, lorn stream, whose sullen tide
    No sedge-crown'd Sisters now attend,
Now waft me from the green hill's side,
    Whose cold turf hides the buried friend!

And see, the fairy valleys fade,
    Dun Night has veil'd the solemn view!
—Yet once again, dear parted shade,
    Meek Nature's child, again adieu!

The genial meads assign'd to bless
    Thy life, shall mourn thy early doom;
Their hinds, and shepherd-girls shall dress
    With simple hands thy rural tomb.

Long, long, thy stone, and pointed clay
    Shall melt the musing Briton's eyes;
O! vales, and wild woods, shall He say
    In yonder grave your Druid lies!

ODE TO SIMPLICITY

O THOU by *Nature* taught,
To breathe her genuine Thought,
In Numbers warmly pure, and sweetly strong:
    Who first on Mountains wild,
    In *Fancy* loveliest Child,
Thy Babe, or *Pleasure's*, nurs'd the Pow'rs of Song!

Thou, who with Hermit Heart
Disdain'st the Wealth of Art,
And Gauds, and pageant Weeds, and trailing Pall:
    But com'st a decent Maid,
    In *Attic* Robe array'd,
O chaste unboastful Nymph, to Thee I call!

By all the honey'd Store
On *Hybla's* Thymy Shore,
By all her Blooms, and mingled Murmurs dear,
By Her whose Love-born Woe
In Ev'ning Musings slow,
Sooth'd sweetly sad *Electra's* Poet's Ear:

By old *Cephisus* deep,
Who spread his wavy Sweep
In warbled Wand'rings round thy green Retreat,
On whose enamelled Side
When holy *Freedom* died
No equal Haunt allur'd thy future Feet.

O Sister meek of Truth,
To my admiring Youth,
Thy sober Aid and native Charms infuse!
The Flow'rs that sweetest breathe,
Tho' Beauty call'd the Wreath,
Still ask thy Hand to range their order'd Hues.

While *Rome* could none esteem
But Virtue's Patriot Theme,
You lov'd her Hills, and led her Laureate Band:
But stayed to sing alone
To one distinguish'd Throne,
And turn'd they Face, and fled her alter'd Land.

No more, in Hall or Bow'r,
The Passions own thy Pow'r,
Love, only Love her forceless Numbers mean:
For Thou hast left her Shrine,
Nor Olive more, nor Vine,
Shall gain thy Feet to bless the servile Scene.

Though Taste, though Genius bless,
To some divine Excess,
Faints the cold Work till Thou inspire the whole;

What each, what all supply,
May court, may charm our Eye,
Thou, only Thou, can'st raise the meeting Soul!

Of These let others ask,
To aid some mighty Task,
I only seek to find thy temperate Vale:
Where oft my Reed might sound
To Maids and Shepherds round,
And all thy sons, O *Nature*, learn my Tale.

ODE TO EVENING

IF ought of Oaten Stop, or Pastoral Song,
May hope, O pensive *Eve*, to sooth thine Ear,
    Like thy own brawling springs,
    Thy Springs, and dying Gales.

O *Nymph* reserv'd, while now the bright-hair'd Sun
Sits in yon western Tent, whose cloudy Skirts,
    With Brede ethereal wove,
    O'erhang his wavy Bed:

Now Air is hush'd, save where the weak-ey'd Bat,
With short shrill Shriek flits by on leathern Wing,
    Or where the Beetle winds
    His small but sullen Horn,

As oft he rises 'midst the twilight Path,
Against the Pilgrim born[e] in heedless Hum:
    Now teach me, *Maid* compos'd,
    To breathe some soften'd Strain,

Whose Numbers stealing thro' thy dark'ning Vale,
May not unseemly with its Stillness suit,
    As musing slow, I hail
    Thy genial lov'd Return!

For when thy folding Star arising shews
His paly Circlet, at his warning Lamp
    The fragrant *Hours*, and *Elves*
    Who slept in Buds the Day,

And many a *Nymph* who wreaths her Brows with Sedge,
And sheds the fresh'ning Dew, and lovelier still,
    The *Pensive Pleasures* sweet
    Prepare thy shadowy Car.

Then let me rove some wild and heathy Scene,
Or find some Ruin, 'midst its dreary Dells,
    Whose Walls more awful nod
    By thy religious Gleams.

Or if chill blust'ring Winds, or driving Rain,
Prevent my willing Feet, be mine the Hut,
    That from the Mountain's Side,
    Views Wilds, and swelling Floods,

And Hamlets brown, and dim-discover'd Spires,
And hears their simple Bell, and marks o'er all
    Thy Dewy Fingers draw
    The gradual dusky Veil.

While *Spring* shall pour his Show'rs, as oft he wont,
And bathe thy breathing Tresses, meekest *Eve*!
    While Summer loves to sport,
    Beneath thy ling'ring Light:

While sallow *Autumn* fills thy lap with Leaves,
Or *Winter*, yelling thro' the troublous Air,
    Affrights thy shrinking Train,
    And rudely rends thy Robes.

So long regardful of thy quiet Rule,
Shall *Fancy, Friendship, Science*, smiling *Peace*,
    Thy gentlest Influence own,
    And love thy fav'rite Name!

MARK AKENSIDE (1721–1770)
INSCRIPTION FOR A GROTTO

To me, who in their lays the shepherds call
Actaea, daughter of the neighbouring stream,
This cave belongs. The fig-tree and the vine,
Which o'er the rocky entrance downward shoot,
Were placed by Glycon. He with cowslips pale,
Primrose, and purple Lychnis, deck'd the green
Before my threshold, and my shelving walls
With honeysuckle cover'd. Here at noon,
Lull'd by the murmur of my rising fount,
I slumber: here my clustering fruits I tend;
Or from the humid flowers, at break of day,
Fresh garlands weave, and chase from all my bounds
Each thing impure or noxious. Enter-in,
O stranger, undismay'd. Nor bat nor toad
Here lurks: and if thy breast of blameless thoughts
Approve thee, not unwelcome shalt thou tread
My quiet mansion: chiefly if thy name
Wise Pallas and the immortal Muses own.

CHRISTOPHER SMART (1722–1771)
From A SONG TO DAVID

DAVID the son of Jesse said, and the man who was raised up on high, the anointed of the God of Jacob, and the sweet Psalmist of Israel, said,
The SPIRIT OF THE LORD spake by me, and HIS WORD was in my tongue.—2 *Sam.* xxiii. 1, 2.

I

O THOU, that sit'st upon a throne,
With harp of high majestic tone,
 To praise the King of Kings;
And voice of heav'n-ascending swell,
Which, while its deeper notes excell,
 Clear, as a clarion, rings:

II

To bless each valley, grove and coast,
And charm the cherubs to the post
   Of gratitude in throngs;
To *keep* the days on Zion's mount,
And send the year to his account,
   With dances and with songs:

III

O Servant of God's holiest charge,
The minister of praise at large,
   Which thou may'st now receive;
From thy blest mansion hail and hear,
From topmost eminence appear
   To this the wreath I weave.

IV

Great, valiant, pious, good, and clean,
Sublime, contemplative, serene,
   Strong, constant, pleasant, wise!
Bright effluence of exceeding grace;
Best man!—the swiftness and the race,
   The peril, and the prize! . . .

XVIII

He sung of God—the mighty source
Of all things—the stupendous force
   On which all strength depends;
From whose right arm, beneath whose eyes,
All period, pow'r, and enterprize
   Commences, reigns, and ends.

XIX

Angels—their ministry and meed,
Which to and fro with blessings speed,
   Or with their citterns wait;
Where Michael with his millions bows,
Where dwells the seraph and his spouse,
   The cherub and her mate.

XX

Of man—the semblance and effect
Of God and Love—the Saint elect
　For infinite applause—
To rule the land, and briny broad,
To be laborious in his laud,
　And heroes in his cause.

XXI

The world—the clust'ring spheres he made,
The glorious light, the soothing shade,
　Dale, champaign, grove, and hill;
The multitudinous abyss,
Where secrecy remains in bliss,
　And wisdom hides her skill.

XXII

Trees, plants, and flow'rs—of virtuous root;
Gem yielding blossom, yielding fruit,
　Choice gums and precious balm;
Bless ye the nosegay in the vale,
And with the sweetness of the gale
　Enrich the thankful psalm.

XXIII

Of fowl—e'en ev'ry beak and wing
Which cheer the winter, hail the spring,
　That live in peace or prey;
They that make music, or that mock,
The quail, the brave domestic cock,
　The raven, swan, and jay.

XXIV

Of fishes—ev'ry size and shape,
Which nature frames of light escape,
　Devouring man to shun:
The shells are in the wealthy deep,
The shoals upon the surface leap,
　And love the glancing sun.

XXV

Of beasts—the beaver plods his task;
While the sleek tigers roll and bask,
  Nor yet the shades arouse:
Her cave the mining coney scoops;
Where o'er the mead the mountain stoops,
  The kids exult and brouse.

XXVI

Of gems—their virtue and their price,
Which hid in earth from man's device,
  Their darts of lustre sheathe;
The jasper of the master's stamp,
The topaz blazing like a lamp
  Among the mines beneath. . . .

LI

For ADORATION all the ranks
Of angels yield eternal thanks,
  And DAVID in the midst;
With God's good poor, which, last and least
In man's esteem, thou to thy feast,
  O blessed bridegroom, bid'st.

LII

For ADORATION seasons change,
And order, truth, and beauty range,
  Adjust, attract, and fill:
The grass the polyanthus cheques;
And polish'd porphyry reflects,
  By the descending rill.

LIII

Rich almonds colour to the prime
For ADORATION; tendrils climb,
  And fruit-trees pledge their gems;

And Ivis [1] with her gorgeous vest
Builds for her eggs her cunning nest,
  And bell-flowers bow their stems.

LIV

With vinous syrup cedars spout;
From rocks pure honey gushing out,
  For ADORATION springs:
All scenes of painting croud the map
Of nature; to the mermaid's pap
  The scaled infant clings.

LV

The spotted ounce and playsome cubs
Run rustling 'mongst the flow'ring shrubs,
  And lizards feed the moss;
For ADORATION beasts embark,
While waves upholding halcyon's ark
  No longer roar and toss. . . .

LXI

The laurels with the winter strive;
The crocus burnishes alive
  Upon the snow-clad earth:
For ADORATION myrtles stay
To keep the garden from dismay,
  And bless the sight from dearth.

LXII

The pheasant shews his pompous neck;
And ermine, jealous of a speck,
  With fear eludes offence:
The sable, with his glossy pride,
For ADORATION is descried,
  Where frosts the waves condense.

[1] Humming-bird.

LXIII

The cheerful holly, pensive yew,
And holy thorn, their trim renew;
　The squirrel hoards his nuts:
All creatures batten o'er their stores,
And careful nature all her doors
　For ADORATION shuts.

LXIV

For ADORATION, DAVID's psalms
Lift up the heart to deeds of alms;
　And he, who kneels and chants,
Prevails his passions to control,
Finds meat and med'cine to the soul,
　Which for translation pants.

LXV

For ADORATION, beyond match,
The scholar bulfinch aims to catch
　The soft flute's iv'ry touch;
And, careless on the hazle spray,
The daring redbreast keeps at bay
　The damsel's greedy clutch.

LXVI

For ADORATION, in the skies,
The Lord's philosopher espies
　The Dog, the Ram, and Rose;
The planet's ring, Orion's sword;
Nor is his greatness less ador'd
　In the vile worm that glows. . . .

LXXII

Sweet is the dew that falls betimes,
And drops upon the leafy limes;
　Sweet Hermon's fragrant air:
Sweet is the lily's silver bell,;
And sweet the wakeful tapers smell
　That watch for early pray'r.

LXXIII

Sweet the young nurse with love intense,
Which smiles o'er sleeping innocence;
  Sweet when the lost arrive:
Sweet the musician's ardour beats,
While his vague mind's in quest of sweets,
  The choicest flow'rs to hive.

LXXIV

Sweeter in all the strains of love,
The language of thy turtle-dove,
  Pair'd to thy swelling chord;
Sweeter with ev'ry grace endu'd,
The glory of thy gratitude,
  Respir'd unto the Lord.

LXXV

Strong is the horse upon his speed;
Strong in pursuit the rapid glede,
  Which makes at once his game:
Strong the tall ostrich on the ground;
Strong thro' the turbulent profound
  Shoots xiphias [1] to his aim.

LXXVI

Strong is the lion—like a coal
His eye-ball—like a bastion's mole
  His chest against the foes:
Strong, the gier-eagle on his sail,
Strong against tide, th' enormous whale
  Emerges as he goes.

LXXVII

But stronger still, in earth and air,
And in the sea, the man of pray'r,
  And far beneath the tide;

[1] The sword-fish.

And in the seat to faith assign'd,
Where ask is have, where seek is find,
  Where knock is open wide.

LXXVIII

Beauteous the fleet before the gale ;
Beauteous the multitudes in mail,
  Rank'd arms and crested heads :
Beauteous the garden's umbrage mild,
Walk, water, meditated wild,
  And all the bloomy beds.

LXXIX

Beauteous the moon full on the lawn ;
And beauteous, when the veil's withdrawn,
  The virgin to her spouse :
Beauteous the temple deck'd and fill'd,
When to the heav'n of heav'ns they build
  Their heart-directed vows.

LXXX

Beauteous, yea beauteous more than these,
The shepherd king upon his knees,
  For his momentous trust ;
With wish of infinite conceit,
For man, beast, mute, the small and great,
  And prostrate dust to dust . . . .

LXXXIV

Glorious the sun in mid career ;
Glorious th' assembled fires appear ;
  Glorious the comet's train :
Glorious the trumpet and alarm ;
Glorious th' almighty stretch'd-out arm.
  Glorious th' enraptur'd main :

LXXXV

Glorious the northern lights astream ;
Glorious the song, when God's the theme ;
 Glorious the thunder's roar :
Glorious hosanna from the den ;
Glorious the catholic amen ;
 Glorious the martyr's gore ;

LXXXVI

Glorious—more glorious is the crown
Of Him that brought salvation down
 By meekness, call'd thy Son ;
Thou that stupendous truth believ'd,
And now the matchless deed's atchiev'd,
 DETERMINED, DARED, and DONE.

JOSEPH WARTON THE YOUNGER
(1722–1800)

AN EPISTLE FROM THOMAS HEARN, *Antiquary*

FRIEND of the moss-grown Spire and crumbling **Arch,**
Who wont'st at Eve to pace the long-lost Bounds
Of lonesome *Osney* ! what malignant Fiend
Thy cloister-loving Mind, from ancient Lore,
Hath base seduc'd ? Urg'd thy apostate Pen
To trench deep Wounds on *Antiquaries* sage,
And drag the venerable Fathers forth,
Victims to Laughter ! Cruel as the Mandate
Of mitred Priests, who *Baskett* late enjoined
To throw aside the reverend Letters *black,*
And print *Fast-Prayers* in *modern* Type !—At this
Leland, and *Willis, Dugdale, Tanner, Wood,*
Illustrious Names ! with *Camden, Aubrey, Lloyd,*
Scald their old Cheeks with Tears ! For once **they**
 hop'd
To seal thee for their own ! And fondly deem'd
The Muses, at thy Call, would crowding come
To deck *Antiquity* with Flowrets gay.

But now may Curses every Search attend
That seems inviting ! May'st thou pore in vain
For dubious Doorways ! May revengeful Moths
Thy Ledgers eat ! May chronologic Spouts
Retain no Cypher legible ! May Crypts
Lurk undiscern'd ! Nor mayst thou spell the Names
Of Saints in storied Windows ! Nor the Dates
Of Bells discover ! Nor the genuine Site
Of Abbots Pantries ! And may *Godstowe* veil,
Deep from thy Eyes profane, her *Gothic* charms !

OLIVER GOLDSMITH (1728–1774)

From RETALIATION

Of old, when Scarron his companions invited,
Each guest brought his dish, and the feast was united ;
If our landlord supplies us with beef, and with fish,
Let each guest bring himself, and he brings the best
    dish :
Our Dean shall be venison, just fresh from the plains ;
Our Burke shall be tongue, with the garnish of brains ;
Our Will shall be wild fowl, of excellent flavour,
And Dick with his pepper, shall heighten their savour :
Our Cumberland's sweetbread its place shall obtain,
And Douglas's pudding substantial and plain :
Our Garrick's a sallad, for in him we see
Oil, vinegar, sugar, and saltness agree :
To make out the dinner full certain I am,
That Ridge is anchovy, and Reynolds is lamb. . . .
    Here lies our good Edmund,[1] whose genius was such,
We scarcely can praise it, or blame it too much ;
Who, born for the Universe, narrow'd his mind,
And to party gave up, what was meant for mankind.
Tho' fraught with all learning, kept straining his throat
To persuade Tommy Townshend to lend him a vote ;
Who, too deep for his hearers, still went on refining,
And thought of convincing, while they thought of dining ;

[1] Edmund Burke.

Tho' equal to all things, for all things unfit;
Too nice for a statesman, too proud for a wit;
For a patriot too cool; for a drudge, disobedient;
And too fond of the *right* to pursue the *expedient*.
In short, 'twas his fate, unemploy'd, or in play, sir,
To eat mutton cold, and cut blocks with a razor. . . .

    Here lies David Garrick, describe him who can,
An abridgment of all that was pleasant in man;
As an actor, confest without rival to shine,
As a wit, if not first, in the very first line,
Yet, with talents like these, and an excellent heart,
The man had his failings—a dupe to his art;
Like an ill judging beauty, his colours he spread,
And be-plaister'd, with rouge, his own natural red.
On the stage he was natural, simple, affecting,
'Twas only that, when he was off, he was acting:
With no reason on earth to go out of his way,
He turn'd and he varied full ten times a day;
Tho' secure of our hearts, yet confoundedly sick
If they were not his own by finessing and trick;
He cast off his friends, as a huntsman his pack,
For he knew when he pleas'd he could whistle them
    back.
Of praise a mere glutton, he swallow'd what came,
And the puff of a dunce, he mistook it for fame;
Till his relish grown callous, almost to disease,
Who pepper'd the highest, was surest to please.
But let us be candid, and speak out our mind,
If dunces applauded, he paid them in kind.
Ye Kenricks, ye Kellys, and Woodfalls so grave,
What a commerce was yours, while you got and you
    gave!
How did Grub-street re-echo the shouts that you
    rais'd,
While he was be-Roscius'd, and you were be-prais'd?
But peace to his spirit, wherever it flies,
To act as an angel, and mix with the skies:
Those poets, who owe their best fame to his skill,
Shall still be his flatterers, go where he will;

Old Shakespeare, receive him, with praise and with love,
And Beaumonts and Bens be his Kellys above. . . .
   Here Reynolds is laid, and, to tell you my mind,
He has not left a wiser or better behind;
His pencil was striking, resistless, and grand;
His manners were gentle, complying and bland;
Still born to improve us in every part,
His pencil our faces, his manners our heart:
To coxcombs averse, yet most civilly steering,
When they judged without skill he was still hard of
    hearing;
When they talk'd of their Raphaels, Correggios, and
    stuff,
He shifted his trumpet, and only took snuff.

From THE DESERTED VILLAGE

Sweet Auburn! loveliest village of the plain,
Where health and plenty cheer'd the labouring swain,
Where smiling spring its earliest visit paid,
And parting summer's lingering blooms delay'd:
Dear lovely bowers of innocence and ease,
Seats of my youth, when every sport could please,
How often have I loiter'd o'er thy green,
Where humble happiness endear'd each scene;
How often have I paus'd on every charm,
The shelter'd cot, the cultivated farm,
The never-failing brook, the busy mill,
The decent church that topp'd the neighbouring hill,
The hawthorn bush, with seats beneath the shade,
For talking age and whisp'ring lovers made;
How often have I bless'd the coming day,
When toil remitting lent its turn to play,
And all the village train, from labour free,
Led up their sports beneath the spreading tree;
While many a pastime circled in the shade,
The young contending as the old survey'd;
And many a gambol frolick'd o'er the ground,
And sleights of art and feats of strength went round;

And still as each repeated pleasure tir'd,
Succeeding sports the mirthful band inspir'd ;
The dancing pair that simply sought renown,
By holding out to tire each other down ;
The swain mistrustless of his smutted face,
While secret laughter tittered round the place ;
The bashful virgin's side-long looks of love,
The matron's glance that would those looks reprove :
These were thy charms, sweet village ; sports like these,
With sweet succession, taught e'en toil to please ;
These round thy bowers their cheerful influence shed,
These were thy charms—But all these charms are fled.

Sweet smiling village, loveliest of the lawn,
Thy sports are fled, and all thy charms withdrawn ;
Amidst thy bowers the tyrant's hand is seen,
And desolation saddens all thy green :
One only master grasps the whole domain,
And half a tillage stints thy smiling plain :
No more thy glassy brook reflects the day,
But chok'd with sedges, works its weedy way.
Along thy glades, a solitary guest,
The hollow-sounding bittern guards its nest ;
Amidst thy desert walks the lapwing flies,
And tires their echoes with unvaried cries.
Sunk are thy bowers in shapeless ruin all,
And the long grass o'ertops the mould'ring wall ;
And trembling, shrinking from the spoiler's hand,
Far, far away, thy children leave the land.

Ill fares the land, to hast'ning ills a prey,
Where wealth accumulates, and men decay :
Princes and lords may flourish, or may fade ;
A breath can make them, as a breath has made ;
But a bold peasantry, their country's pride,
When once destroy'd, can never be supplied.

A time there was, ere England's griefs began,
When every rood of ground maintain'd its man ;
For him light labour spread her wholesome store,
Just gave what life requir'd, but gave no more :
His best companions, innocence and health ;
And his best riches, ignorance of wealth.

But times are alter'd ; trade's unfeeling train
Usurp the land and dispossess the swain ;
Along the lawn, where scatter'd hamlets rose,
Unwieldy wealth, and cumbrous pomp repose ;
And every want to opulence allied,
And every pang that folly pays to pride.
Those gentle hours that plenty bade to bloom,
Those calm desires that ask'd but little room,
Those healthful sports that grac'd the peaceful scene,
Liv'd in each look, and brighten'd all the green ;
These, far departing, seek a kinder shore,
And rural mirth and manners are no more.

Sweet AUBURN ! parent of the blissful hour,
Thy glades forlorn confess the tyrant's power.
Here as I take my solitary rounds,
Amidst thy tangling walks, and ruin'd grounds,
And, many a year elaps'd, return to view
Where once the cottage stood, the hawthorn grew,
Remembrance wakes with all her busy train,
Swells at my breast, and turns the past to pain.

In all my wand'rings round this world of care,
In all my griefs—and GOD has given my share—
I still had hopes my latest hours to crown,
Amidst these humble bowers to lay me down ;
To husband out life's taper at the close,
And keep the flame from wasting by repose.
I still had hopes, for pride attends us still,
Amidst the swains to show my book-learn'd skill,
Around my fire an evening group to draw,
And tell of all I felt, and all I saw ;

And, as a hare, whom hounds and horns pursue,
Pants to the place from whence at first she flew,
I still had hopes, my long vexations pass'd,
Here to return—and die at home at last. . . .

    Near yonder copse, where once the garden smil'd,
And still where many a garden flower grows wild;
There, where a few torn shrubs the place disclose,
The village preacher's modest mansion rose.
A man he was to all the country dear,
And passing rich with forty pounds a year;
Remote from towns he ran his godly race,
Nor e'er had chang'd, nor wish'd to change his place;
Unpractis'd he to fawn, or seek for power,
By doctrines fashion'd to the varying hour;
Far other aims his heart had learned to prize,
More skill'd to raise the wretched than to rise.
His house was known to all the vagrant train,
He chid their wand'rings, but reliev'd their pain;
The long-remember'd beggar was his guest,
Whose beard descending swept his aged breast;
The ruin'd spendthrift, now no longer proud,
Claim'd kindred there, and had his claims allow'd.
The broken soldier, kindly bade to stay,
Sat by his fire, and talk'd the night away;
Wept o'er his wounds, or tales of sorrow done,
Shoulder'd his crutch, and show'd how fields were won.
Pleas'd with his guests, the good man learned to glow,
And quite forgot their vices in their woe;
Careless their merits, or their faults to scan,
His pity gave ere charity began.

    Thus to relieve the wretched was his pride,
And e'en his failings lean'd to Virtue's side;
But in his duty prompt at every call,
He watch'd and wept, he pray'd and felt, for all.
And, as a bird each fond endearment tries
To tempt its new-fledg'd offspring to the skies,

He tried each art, reprov'd each dull delay,
Allur'd to brighter worlds, and led the way.

    Beside the bed where parting life was laid,
And sorrow, guilt, and pain, by turns dismay'd,
The reverend champion stood. At his control,
Despair and anguish fled the struggling soul ;
Comfort came down the trembling wretch to raise,
And his last falt'ring accents whisper'd praise.

    At church, with meek and unaffected grace,
His looks adorn'd the venerable place ;
Truth from his lips prevail'd with double sway,
And fools, who came to scoff, remain'd to pray.
The service pass'd, around the pious man,
With steady zeal, each honest rustic ran ;
Even children follow'd with endearing wile,
And pluck'd his gown, to share the good man's smile.
His ready smile a parent's warmth express'd,
Their welfare pleas'd him, and their cares distress'd ;
To them his heart, his love, his griefs were given,
But all his serious thoughts had rest in Heaven.
As some tall cliff, that lifts its awful form,
Swells from the vale, and midway leaves the storm,
Though round its breast the rolling clouds are spread,
Eternal sunshine settles on its head.

    Beside yon straggling fence that skirts the way,
With blossom'd furze unprofitable gay,
There, in his noisy mansion, skill'd to rule,
The village master taught his little school ;
A man severe he was, and stern to view ;
I knew him well, and every truant knew ;
Well had the boding tremblers learn'd to trace
The day's disasters in his morning face ;
Full well they laugh'd, with counterfeited glee,
At all his jokes, for many a joke had he ;
Full well the busy whisper, circling round,
Convey'd the dismal tidings when he frown'd :

Yet he was kind ; or if severe in aught,
The love he bore to learning was in fault ;
The village all declar'd how much he knew ;
'Twas certain he could write, and cypher too ;
Lands he could measure, terms and tides presage,
And e'en the story ran that he could gauge.
In arguing too, the parson own'd his skill,
For e'en though vanquish'd, he could argue still ;
While words of learned length and thund'ring sound
Amazed the gazing rustics rang'd around,
And still they gaz'd and still the wonder grew,
That one small head could carry all he knew.

    But past is all his fame. The very spot
Where many a time he triumph'd, is forgot.
Near yonder thorn, that lifts its head on high,
Where once the sign-post caught the passing eye,
Low lies that house where nut-brown draughts inspir'd,
Where grey-beard mirth and smiling toil retir'd,
Where village statesmen talk'd with looks profound,
And news much older than their ale went round.
Imagination fondly stoops to trace
The parlour splendours of that festive place ;
The white-wash'd wall, the nicely sanded floor,
The varnish'd clock that click'd behind the door ;
The chest contrived a double debt to pay,
A bed by night, a chest of drawers by day ;
The pictures plac'd for ornament and use,
The twelve good rules, the royal game of goose ;
The hearth, except when winter chill'd the day,
With aspen boughs, and flowers, and fennel gay ;
While broken tea-cups, wisely kept for show,
Rang'd o'er the chimney, glisten'd in a row. . . .

    Ye friends to truth, ye statesmen, who survey
The rich man's joys increase, the poor's decay,
'Tis yours to judge, how wide the limits stand
Between a splendid and a happy land.

Proud swells the tide with loads of freighted ore,
And shouting Folly hails them from her shore;
Hoards, e'en beyond the miser's wish abound,
And rich men flock from all the world around.
Yet count our gains. This wealth is but a name
That leaves our useful products still the same.
Not so the loss. The man of wealth and pride
Takes up a space that many poor supplied;
Space for his lake, his park's extended bounds,
Space for his horses, equipage, and hounds;
The robe that wraps his limbs in silken sloth
Has robb'd the neighbouring fields of half their growth,
His seat, where solitary sports are seen,
Indignant spurns the cottage from the green;
Around the world each needful product flies,
For all the luxuries the world supplies:
While thus the land adorn'd for pleasure, all
In barren splendour feebly waits the fall. . . .

E'en now the devastation is begun,
And half the business of destruction done;
E'en now, methinks, as pond'ring here I stand,
I see the rural virtues leave the land:
Down where yon anchoring vessel spreads the sail,
That idly waiting flaps with ev'ry gale,
Downward they move, a melancholy band,
Pass from the shore, and darken all the strand.
Contented toil, and hospitable care,
And kind connubial tenderness, are there;
And piety, with wishes plac'd above,
And steady loyalty, and faithful love.
And thou, sweet Poetry, thou loveliest maid,
Still first to fly where sensual joys invade;
Unfit in these degenerate times of shame,
To catch the heart, or strike for honest fame;
Dear charming nymph, neglected and decried,
My shame in crowds, my solitary pride;
Thou source of all my bliss, and all my woe,
That found'st me poor at first, and keep'st me so;

Thou guide by which the nobler arts excel,
Thou nurse of every virtue, fare thee well!
Farewell, and Oh! where'er thy voice be tried,
On Torno's cliffs, or Pambamarca's side,
Whether where equinoctial fervours glow,
Or winter wraps the polar world in snow,
Still let thy voice, prevailing over time,
Redress the rigours of th' inclement clime;
Aid slighted truth; with thy persuasive strain
Teach erring man to spurn the rage of gain;
Teach him, that states of native strength possess'd,
Though very poor, may still be very bless'd;
That trade's proud empire hastes to swift decay
As ocean sweeps the labour'd mole away;
While self-dependent power can time defy,
As rocks resist the billows and the sky.

THE RT. HON. JUSTICE SIR JAMES MARRIOTT
(?1730–1803)
CANZONETTA

Soft slept the sea within its silver bed.
    To the scarce breathing gale
        The silken sail
    With vent'rous hands I spread:
And saw the rocks, and passed; yet felt no fear!
All danger distant seemed; which was, alas, too near!

    Love, calm deceiver! seated by my side,
        His secret fraud enjoyed!
        Too oft employed
    In sport my bark to guide!
We reached the port. The little Pilot smiled.
" Can Love deceive ? " I said, and kissed the laugh-
    ing Child.

He clapped his wings ; and lightly, through the air,
Flew from my longing eyes.
  The storms arise,
  And back my vessel bear,
Secure what port can hapless Lovers meet ?
We blame the winds and seas ; yet clasp the dear deceit !

CHARLES CHURCHILL (1731–1764)

From " THE GHOST "

Book II

POMPOSO [1] (insolent and loud),
Vain idol of a *scribbling* crowd,
Whose very name inspires an awe,
Whose ev'ry word is Sense and Law,
For what his Greatness hath decreed,
Like Laws of *Persia* and of *Mede*,
Sacred thro' all the realm of *Wit*,
Must never of Repeal admit ;
Who, cursing flatt'ry, is the tool
Of ev'ry fawning, flatt'ring fool ;
Who wit with jealous eye surveys,
And sickens at another's praise ;
Who, proudly seiz'd of *Learning's* throne,
Now damns all Learning but his own ;
Who scorns those common wares to trade in,
Reas'ning, *Convincing*, and *Persuading*,
But makes each sentence current pass
With *Puppy, Coxcomb, Scoundrel, Ass* ;
For 'tis with him a certain rule,
The Folly's prov'd when he calls Fool ;
Who, to increase his native strength,
Draws words six syllables in length,
With which, assisted with a frown
By way of Club, he knocks us down ;

[1] Dr. Johnson.

Who 'bove the Vulgar dares to rise,
And Sense of *Decency* defies,
(For this same *Decency* is made
Only for Bunglers in the trade,
And, like the *Cobweb Laws*, is still
Broke thro' by *Great ones* when they will)—
Pomposo, with *strong sense* supplied,
Supported, and confirm'd by *Pride*,
His Comrades' terrors to beguile,
Grinn'd horribly a ghastly smile :
Features so horrid, were it light,
Would put the Devil himself to flight.

· · · ·

From " GOTHAM," Book II

THE *First*,[1] who, from his native soil remov'd,
Held *England's* sceptre, a tame Tyrant prov'd.
Virtue he lack'd, curs'd with those thoughts which
   spring
In souls of vulgar stamp, to be a King ;
Spirit he had not, tho' he laugh'd at Laws,
To play the bold-fac'd Tyrant with applause ;
On practices most mean he rais'd his pride,
And Craft oft gave, what Wisdom oft denied.
Ne'er could he feel how truly Man is blest
In blessing those around him ; in his breast,
Crowded with follies, Honour found no room ;
Mark'd for a Coward in his Mother's Womb,
He was too proud without affronts to live,
Too timorous to punish or forgive.
  To gain a crown, which had in course of time,
By fair descent, been his without a crime,
He bore a Mother's exile ; to secure
A greater crown, he basely could endure
The spilling of her blood by foreign knife,
Nor dar'd revenge her death who gave him life ;

[1] James I.

Nay, by fond fear, and fond ambition led,
Struck hands with Those by whom her blood was
   shed.
   Call'd up to Pow'r, scarce warm on England's throne,
He fill'd her Court with beggars from his own,
Turn where You would, the eye with *Scots* was caught,
Or *English* knaves who would be *Scotsmen* thought.
To vain expence unbounded loose he gave,
The dupe of Minions, and of slaves the slave;
On false pretences mighty sums he rais'd,
And damn'd those senates rich, whom, poor, he prais'd:
From Empire thrown, and doom'd to beg her bread,
On foreign bounty whilst a Daughter fed,
He lavish'd sums, for her receiv'd, on Men
Whose names would fix dishonour on my pen.
   Lies were his Play-things, Parliaments his sport,
Book-worms and Catamites engross'd the Court;
Vain of the Scholar, like all *Scotsmen* since
The *Pedant* Scholar, he forgot the Prince,
And, having with some trifles stor'd his brain,
Ne'er learn'd, or wish'd to learn the arts to reign.
Enough he knew to make him vain and proud,
Mock'd by the wise, the wonder of the croud;
False Friend, false Son, false Father, and false King,
False Wit, false Statesman, and false ev'rything,
When He should act, he idly chose to prate,
And pamphlets wrote, when he should save the State.
   Religious, if Religion holds in whim,
To talk with all, he let all talk with him,
Not on God's honour, but his own intent,
Not for Religion sake, but argument;
More vain if some sly, artful, *High-Dutch* slave,
Or, from the *Jesuit* school, some precious knave
Conviction feign'd, than if, to Peace restor'd
By his full soldiership, Worlds hail'd him lord.
   Pow'r was his wish, unbounded as his will,
The Pow'r, without controul, of doing ill.
But what he wish'd, what he made *Bishops* preach,
And *Statesmen* warrant, hung within his reach

He dar'd not seize ; Fear gave, to gall his pride,
That Freedom to the Realm his will denied.
  Of Treaties fond, o'erweening of his parts,
In ev'ry Treaty, of his own mean arts
He fell the dupe ; Peace was his Coward care,
E'en at a time when Justice call'd for war ;
His pen he'd draw, to prove his lack of wit,
But, rather than unsheath the sword, submit ;
Truth fairly must record, and, pleas'd to live
In league with *Mercy*, *Justice* may forgive
Kingdoms betray'd, and Worlds resign'd to *Spain*,
But never can forgive a *Raleigh* slain.
  At length, (with white let Freedom mark that year)
Not fear'd by those, whom most he wish'd to fear,
Not loved by those, whom most he wish'd to love,
He went to answer for his faults above,
To answer to that God, from whom alone
He claim'd to hold, and to abuse the throne,
Leaving behind, a curse to all his line,
The bloody Legacy of *Right Divine*.

From " THE CANDIDATE "

  ENOUGH of *Self*—that darling, luscious theme,
O'er which Philosophers in raptures dream ;
On which with seeming disregard they write,
Then prizing most, when most they seem to slight ;
Vain proof of Folly tinctur'd strong with pride !
What Man can from himself himself divide ?
For Me (nor dare I lie) my leading aim,
(Conscience first satisfied) is love of Fame,
Some little Fame deriv'd from some brave few,
Who, prizing Honour, prize her Vot'ries too.
Let All (nor shall resentment flush my cheek)
Who know me well, what they know, freely speak,
So Those (the greatest curse I meet below)
Who know me not, may not pretend to know.
Let none of Those, whom bless'd with parts above
My feeble Genius, still I dare to love,

Doing more mischief than a thousand foes,
Posthumous nonsense to the world expose,
And call it mine, for mine tho' never known,
Or which, if mine, I living blush'd to own.
Know all the World, no greedy heir shall find,
Die when I will, one couplet left behind.
Let none of Those, whom I despise tho' great,
Pretending Friendship to give malice weight,
Publish my life ; let no false, sneaking peer,
(Some such there are) to win the public ear,
Hand me to shame with some vile anecdote,
Nor soul-gall'd Bishop damn me with a note.
Let one poor sprig of Bay around my head
Bloom whilst I live, and point me out when dead ;
Let It (may Heav'n, indulgent, grant that pray'r)
Be planted on my grave, nor wither there ;
And when, on travel bound, some riming guest
Roams thro the Church-yard, whilst his Dinner's dress'd,
Let It hold up this comment to his eyes ;
Life to the last enjoy'd, *here* Churchill lies ;
Whilst (O, what joy that pleasing flatt'ry gives)
Reading my Works, he cries—*here* Churchill lives.

WILLIAM COWPER
(1731–1800)
THE DIVERTING HISTORY OF JOHN GILPIN :
SHOWING HOW HE WENT FARTHER THAN HE INTENDED, AND CAME SAFE HOME AGAIN

JOHN GILPIN was a citizen
  Of credit and renown ;
A trainband captain eke was he
  Of famous London town.

John Gilpin's spouse said to her dear,
  " Though wedded we have been
These twice ten tedious years, yet we
  No holiday have seen.

"To-morrow is our wedding-day,
   And we will then repair
Unto the Bell at Edmonton,
   All in a chaise and pair.

"My sister and my sister's child,
   Myself and children three,
Will fill the chaise; so you must ride
   On horseback after we."

He soon replied, "I do admire
   Of womankind but one,
And you are she, my dearest dear;
   Therefore it shall be done.

"I am a linendraper bold,
   As all the world doth know;
And my good friend the calender
   Will lend his horse to go."

Quoth Mrs. Gilpin, "That's well said;
   And for that wine is dear,
We will be furnished with our own,
   Which is both bright and clear."

John Gilpin kissed his loving wife;
   O'erjoyed was he to find,
That, though on pleasure she was bent,
   She had a frugal mind.

The morning came, the chaise was brought,
   But yet was not allowed
To drive up to the door, lest all
   Should say that she was proud.

So three doors off the chaise was stayed,
   Where they did all get in;
Six precious souls, and all agog
   To dash through thick and thin.

Smack went the whip, round went the wheels,
  Were never folk so glad;
The stones did rattle underneath,
  As if Cheapside were mad.

John Gilpin at his horse's side
  Seized fast the flowing mane;
And up he got in haste to ride,
  But soon came down again:

For saddletree scarce reached had he,
  His journey to begin,
When, turning round his head, he saw
  Three customers come in.

So down he came; for loss of time,
  Although it grieved him sore,
Yet loss of pence full well he knew,
  Would trouble him much more. . . .

Now see him mounted once again
  Upon his nimble steed,
Full slowly pacing o'er the stones,
  With caution and good heed.

But finding soon a smoother road
  Beneath his well-shod feet,
The snorting beast began to trot,
  Which galled him in his seat.

So, " Fair and softly," John he cried,
  But John he cried in vain;
That trot became a gallop soon,
  In spite of curb and rein.

So stooping down, as needs he must
  Who cannot sit upright,
He grasped the mane with both his hands,
  And eke with all his might.

His horse, who never in that sort
  Had handled been before,
What thing upon his back had got,
  Did wonder more and more.

Away went Gilpin, neck or naught ;
  Away went hat and wig :
He little dreamt, when he set out,
  Of running such a rig.

The wind did blow, the cloak did fly,
  Like streamer long and gay,
Till, loop and button failing both,
  At last it flew away.

Then might all people well discern
  The bottles he had slung ;
A bottle swinging at each side,
  As hath been said or sung.

The dogs did bark, the children screamed,
  Up flew the windows all ;
And every soul cried out, " Well done ! "
  As loud as he could bawl.

Away went Gilpin—who but he ?
  His fame soon spread around ;
" He carries weight ! he rides a race !
  'Tis for a thousand pound ! "

And still, as fast as he drew near,
  'Twas wonderful to view,
How in a trice the turnpike men
  Their gates wide open threw. . . .

And now, as he went bowing down
  His reeking head full low,
The bottles twain behind his back
  Were shattered at a blow. . . .

At Edmonton his loving wife
  From the balcony spied
Her tender husband, wondering much
  To see how he did ride.

" Stop, stop, John Gilpin ! here's the house,"
  They all at once did cry ;
" The dinner waits, and we are tired " ;
  Said Gilpin, " So am I ! "

But yet his horse was not a whit
  Inclined to tarry there :
For why ?—his owner had a house
  Full ten miles off, at Ware.

So like an arrow swift he flew,
  Shot by an archer strong ;
So did he fly—which brings me to
  The middle of my song. . . .

Said John, " It is my wedding-day,
  And all the world would stare
If wife should dine at Edmonton,
  And I should dine at Ware."

So turning to his horse he said,
  " I am in haste to dine ;
'Twas for your pleasure you came here,
  You shall go back for mine."

Ah, luckless speech, and bootless boast !
  For which he paid full dear ;
For, while he spake, a braying ass
  Did sing full loud and clear :

Whereat his horse did snort, as he
  Had heard a lion roar,
And galloped off with all his might,
  As he had done before.

Away went Gilpin, and away
 Went Gilpin's hat and wig:
He lost them sooner than at first;
 For why?—They were too big. . . .

Six gentlemen upon the road,
 Thus seeing Gilpin fly,
With postboy scampering in the rear,
 They raised the hue and cry,

"Stop thief! Stop thief! a highwayman!"
 Not one of them was mute;
And all and each that passed that way,
 Did join in the pursuit.

And now the turnpike gates again
 Flew open in short space;
The toll-men thinking as before,
 That Gilpin rode a race.

And so he did, and won it too,
 For he got first to town;
Nor stopped till where he had got up
 He did again get down.

Now let us sing, long live the king,
 And Gilpin long live he;
And when he next doth ride abroad,
 May I be there to see!

ON THE LOSS OF THE *ROYAL GEORGE*

Toll for the brave!
 The brave that are no more!
All sunk beneath the wave,
 Fast by their native shore!

Eight hundred of the brave,
  Whose courage well was tried,
Had made the vessel heel,
  And laid her on her side.

A land breeze shook the shrouds,
  And she was overset;
Down went the Royal George,
  With all her crew complete.

Toll for the brave!
  Brave Kempenfelt is gone;
His last sea-fight is fought,
  His work of glory done.

It was not in the battle;
  No tempest gave the shock;
She sprang no fatal leak;
  She ran upon no rock.

His sword was in its sheath;
  His fingers held the pen,
When Kempenfelt went down
  With twice four hundred men.

Weigh the vessel up,
  Once dreaded by our foes!
And mingle with our cup
  The tear that England owes.

Her timbers yet are sound,
  And she may float again
Full charged with England's thunder,
  And plough the distant main.

But Kempenfelt is gone
  His victories are o'er;
And he and his eight hundred
  Shall plough the wave no more.

ON THE RECEIPT OF MY MOTHER'S PICTURE

O, THAT those lips had language!—Life has passed
With me but roughly since I heard thee last.
Those lips are thine—thy own sweet smile I see,
The same, that oft in childhood solaced me:
Voice only fails; else how distinct they say,
"Grieve not, my child; chase all thy fears away!"
The meek intelligence of those dear eyes
(Bless'd be the art that can immortalize,
The art that baffles time's tyrannic claim
To quench it,) here shines on me still the same.
   Faithful remembrancer of one so dear,
O, welcome guest, though unexpected here!
Who bidd'st me honour with an artless song,
Affectionate, a mother lost so long.
I will obey, not willingly alone,
But gladly, as the precept were her own:
And, while that face renews my filial grief,
Fancy shall weave a charm for my relief,
Shall steep me in Elysian reverie,
A momentary dream that thou art she.
   My mother! when I learn'd that thou wast dead,
Say, wast thou conscious of the tears I shed?
Hovered thy spirit o'er thy sorrowing son,
Wretch even then, life's journey just begun?
Perhaps thou gav'st me, though unfelt, a kiss;
Perhaps a tear, if souls can weep in bliss;
Ah, that maternal smile! it answers, Yes.
I heard the bell tolled on thy burial-day,
I saw the hearse that bore thee slow away,
And, turning from my nursery window, drew
A long, long sigh, and wept a last adieu;
But was it such?—It was. Where thou art gone,
Adieus and farewells are a sound unknown:
May I but meet thee on that peaceful shore,
The parting word shall pass my lips no more!
Thy maidens, grieved themselves at my concern,
Oft gave me promise of thy quick return.

What ardently I wished, I long believed;
And, disappointed still, was still deceived;
By expectation every day beguiled,
Dupe of *to-morrow* even from a child!
Thus many a sad to-morrow came and went,
Till, all my stock of infant sorrow spent,
I learn'd at last submission to my lot,
But though I less deplored thee, ne'er forgot.

SONNET TO MRS. UNWIN

MARY! I want a lyre with other strings,
Such aid from Heaven as some have feign'd they
    drew,
An eloquence scarce given to mortals, new
And undebased by praise of meaner things;
That, ere through age or woe I shed my wings,
I may record thy worth with honour due,
In verse as musical as thou art true,
And that immortalizes whom it sings.
But thou hast little need: there is a book
By seraphs writ with beams of heavenly light,
On which the eyes of God not rarely look,
A chronicle of actions just and bright;
There all thy deeds, my faithful Mary, shine;
And, since thou own'st that praise, I spare thee
    mine.

LOVEST THOU ME?

HARK, my soul! it is the Lord;
'Tis thy Saviour, hear his word;
Jesus speaks, and speaks to thee,
" Say, poor sinner, lovest thou me?

" I delivered thee when bound,
And, when bleeding, healed thy wound,
Sought thee wandering, set thee right,
Turned thy darkness into light.

" Can a woman's tender care
Cease towards the child she bare ?
Yes, she may forgetful be,
Yet will I remember thee.

" Mine is an unchanging love,
Higher than the heights above,
Deeper than the depths beneath,
Free and faithful, strong as death.

" Thou shalt see my glory soon,
When the work of grace is done ;
Partner of my throne shall be :—
Say, poor sinner, lovest thou me ? "

Lord, it is my chief complaint
That my love is weak and faint ;
Yet I love thee and adore,—
Oh ! for grace to love thee more !

From THE TASK

       . . . Scenes that soothed
Or charmed me young, no longer young, I find
Still soothing, and of power to charm me still.
And witness, dear companion of my walks,
Whose arm this twentieth winter I perceive
Fast locked in mine, with pleasure such as love,
Confirmed by long experience of thy worth
And well-tried virtues, could alone inspire—
Witness a joy that thou hast doubled long :
Thou know'st my praise of nature most sincere,
And that my raptures are not conjured up
To serve occasions of poetic pomp,
But genuine, and art partner of them all.
How oft upon yon eminence our pace
Has slackened to a pause, and we have borne
The ruffling wind, scarce conscious that it blew,
While Admiration, feeding at the eye,

And still unsated, dwelt upon the scene.
Thence with what pleasure have we just discerned
The distant plough slow moving, and beside
His labouring team, that swerved not from the track,
The sturdy swain diminished to a boy!
Here, Ouse, slow winding through a level plain
Of spacious meads with cattle sprinkled o'er,
Conducts the eye along his sinuous course
Delighted. There, fast rooted in their bank,
Stand, never overlooked, our favourite elms,
That screen the herdman's solitary hut;
While far beyond, and overthwart the stream,
That, as with molten glass, inlays the vale,
The sloping land recedes into the clouds;
Displaying on its varied side the grace
Of hedge-row beauties numberless, square tower,
Tall spire, from which the sound of cheerful bells
Just undulates upon the listening ear.
Groves, heaths, and smoking villages, remote.
Scenes must be beautiful, which daily viewed
Please daily, and whose novelty survives
Long knowledge and the scrutiny of years:
Praise justly due to those that I describe.
   Nor rural sights alone, but rural sounds,
Exhilarate the spirit, and restore
The tone of languid Nature. Mighty winds
That sweep the skirt of some far-spreading wood
Of ancient growth, make music not unlike
The dash of Ocean on his winding shore,
And lull the spirit while they fill the mind;
Unnumbered branches waving in the blast,
And all their leaves fast fluttering, all at once.
Nor less composure waits upon the roar
Of distant floods, or on the softer voice
Of neighbouring fountain, or of rills that slip
Through the cleft rock, and chiming as they fall
Upon loose pebbles, lose themselves at length
In matted grass, that with a livelier green
Betrays the secret of their silent course.

Nature inanimate employs sweet sounds,
But animated Nature sweeter still,
To sooth and satisfy the human ear.
Ten thousand warblers cheer the day, and one
The livelong night; nor these alone, whose notes
Nice-fingered Art must emulate in vain
But cawing rooks, and kites that swim sublime
In still repeated circles, screaming loud
The jay, the pie and e'en the boding owl
That hails the rising moon, have charms for me
Sounds inharmonious in themselves and harsh
Yet heard in scenes where peace for ever reigns
And only there please highly for their sake. . . .

*

O, Winter, ruler of the inverted year,
Thy scattered hair with sleet like ashes filled,
Thy breath congealed upon thy lips, thy cheeks
Fringed with a beard made white with other snows
Than those of age, thy forehead wrapped in clouds,
A leafless branch thy sceptre, and thy throne
A sliding car, indebted to no wheels,
But urged by storms along its slippery way,
I love thee, all unlovely as thou seem'st,
And dreaded as thou art! Thou hold'st the sun
A prisoner in the yet undawning east,
Shortening his journey between morn and noon,
And hurrying him, impatient of his stay,
Down to the rosy west; but kindly still
Compensating his loss with added hours
Of social converse and instructive ease,
And gathering, at short notice, in one group
The family dispersed, and fixing thought,
Not less dispersed, by daylight and its cares.
I crown thee king of intimate delights,
Fireside enjoyments, homeborn happiness,
And all the comforts that the lowly roof
Of undisturbed retirement, and the hours
Of long uninterrupted evening, know.

No rattling wheels stop short before these gates;
No powdered pert proficient in the art
Of sounding an alarm, assaults these doors
Till the street rings; no stationary steeds
Cough their own knell, while, heedless of the sound,
The silent circle fan themselves, and quake:
But here the needle plies its busy task,
The pattern grows, the well-depicted flower,
Wrought patiently into the snowy lawn,
Unfolds its bosom; buds, and leaves, and sprigs,
And curling tendrils, gracefully disposed,
Follow the nimble finger of the fair;
A wreath, that cannot fade, of flowers that blow
With most success when all besides decay. . . .

*

Forth goes the woodman, leaving unconcerned
The cheerful haunts of man, to wield the axe
And drive the wedge in yonder forest drear,
From morn to eve his solitary task.
Shaggy, and lean, and shrewd, with pointed ears,
And tail cropped short, half lurcher and half cur,
His dog attends him: close behind his heel
Now creeps he slow; and now, with many a frisk
Wide scampering, snatches up the drifted snow
With ivory teeth, or ploughs it with his snout,
Then shakes his powdered coat, and barks for joy.
Heedless of all his pranks, the sturdy churl
Moves right toward the mark; nor stops for aught
But now and then with pressure of his thumb
To' adjust the fragrant charge of a short tube,
That fumes beneath his nose: the trailing cloud
Streams far behind him, scenting all the air.
Now from the roost, or from the neighbouring pale,
Where, diligent to catch the first faint gleam
Of smiling day, they gossiped side by side,
Come trooping at the housewife's well-known call
The feathered tribes domestic: half on wing,
And half on foot, they brush the fleecy flood,

Conscious, and fearful of too deep a plunge.
The sparrows peep, and quit the sheltering eaves
To seize the fair occasion ; well they eye
The scattered grain, and thievishly resolved
To' escape the' impending famine, often scared
As oft return, a pert, voracious kind.
Clean riddance quickly made, one only care
Remains to each—the search of sunny nook,
Or shed impervious to the blast : resigned
To sad necessity, the cock foregoes
His wonted strut ; and, wading at their head
With well-considered steps, seems to resent
His altered gait and stateliness retrenched.
How find the myriads that in summer cheer
The hills and valleys with their ceaseless songs,
Due sustenance, or where subsist they now ?
Earth yields them naught ; the' imprisoned worm is safe
Beneath the frozen clod ; all seeds of herbs
Lie covered close ; and berry-bearing thorns,
That feed the thrush, (whatever some suppose,)
Afford the smaller minstrels no supply.
The long-protracted rigour of the year
Thins all their numerous flocks : in chinks and holes
Ten thousand seek an unmolested end,
As instinct prompts, self-buried ere they die. . . .

★

From dearth to plenty, and from death to life,
Is Nature's progress, when she lectures man
In heavenly truth ; evincing, as she makes
The grand transition, that there lives and works
A soul in all things, and that soul is God.
The beauties of the wilderness are his,
That make so gay the solitary place,
Where no eye sees them : and the fairer forms,
That cultivation glories in, are his.
He sets the bright procession on its way,
And marshals all the order of the year:

He marks the bounds which winter may not pass,
And blunts his pointed fury : in its case,
Russet and rude, folds up the tender germ,
Uninjured, with inimitable art ;
And, ere one flowery season fades and dies,
Designs the blooming wonders of the next.

WILLIAM JULIUS MICKLE (1735–1788)
THE MARINER'S WIFE

BUT are you sure, the news is true ?
  And are you sure, he's well ?
Is this a time to think o' wark ?
  Ye jades ! fling by your Wheel !
    There's nae luck about the house
      There's nae luck at a' !
    There's nae luck about the house
      When our Gudeman's awa' !

Is this a time to think of wark,
  When Colin's at the door ?
Rax me my cloak ! I'll down the Key,
  And see him come ashore !

Rise up, and make a clean fireside !
  Put on the muckle pat !
Gie little Kate her cotton gown ;
  And Jock his Sunday's coat !

Make their shoon as black as slaes,
  Their stockings white as snaw !
It's a' to pleasure our Gudeman,
  He likes to see them braw !

There are twa hens into the crib,
  Have fed this month and mair ;
Make haste, and thraw their necks about,
  That Colin well may fare !

Bring down to me my bigonet!
  My bishop-satin gown!
And then gae tell the Bailie's Wife,
  That Colin's come to town!

My Turkey slippers I'll put on,
  My stockings pearl-blue!
And a' to pleasure our Gudeman!
  For he's baith leal and true!

Sae sweet his voice, sae smooth his tongue,
  His breath's like cauler air!
His very tread has music in't,
  As he comes up the stair! . . .

And will I see his face again?
  And will I hear him speak?
I'm downright dizzy with the joy!
  In troth! I'm like to greet!
    There's nae luck about the house!
      There's nae luck at a'!
    There's nae luck about the house
      When our Gudeman's awa'!

CHARLES DIBDIN (1745–1814)
TOM BOWLING'S EPITAPH

HERE, a sheer hulk, lies poor Tom Bowling,
  The darling of our crew!
No more he'll hear the tempest howling;
  For Death has broached him to.
His form was of the manliest beauty!
  His heart was kind and soft!
Faithful below, he did his duty;
  And now he's gone aloft!

Tom never from his word departed,
  His virtues were so rare!
His friends were many and true-hearted;
  His Poll was kind and fair!

And then he'd sing so blithe and jolly,
  Ah! many's the time and oft!
But mirth is turned to melancholy;
  For Tom is gone aloft!

Yet shall poor Tom find pleasant weather,
  When He, who all commands,
Shall give, to call Life's crew together,
  The word to " pipe all hands "!
Thus Death, who Kings and Tars dispatches,
  In vain Tom's life has doffed!
For, though his body's under hatches,
  His soul is gone aloft!

LADY ANNE BARNARD (1750–1825)
AULD ROBIN GRAY

WHEN the sheep are in the fauld, and the ky at hame,
And a' the warld to sleep are gane,
The waes of my heart fa' in showers frae my eye,
When my Gudeman lyes sound by me.

Young Jemmy loo'd me well, and he sought me for his Bride;
But saving a crown, he had naething beside!
To make that crown a pound, my Jemmy gade to sea;
And the crown and the pound were baith for me!

He had nae been awa' a week but only twa,
When my mother she fell sick, and the cow was stoun awa';
My father brake his arm, and my Jemmy at the sea,
And auld Robin Gray came a-courting me.

My father couldna work, and my mother couldna spin.
I toiled day and night; but their bread I couldna win!

Auld Rob maintain'd them baith ; and, wi' tears in his ee,
Said "Jenny! for their sakes, O, marry me!"

My heart, it said "Nay!" I looked for Jemmy back;
But the wind it blew high, and the ship it was a wreck.
The ship it was a wreck, why didna Jemmy die?
And why do I live to say "Wae's me!"?

Auld Robin argued fair. Tho' my mother didna speak;
She looked in my face, till my heart was like to break!
So they gi'ed him my hand, tho' my heart was in the sea;
And auld Robin Gray is Gudeman to me.

I hadna been a wife a week but only four,
When, sitting sae mournfully at the door,
I saw my Jemmy's wraith; for I coudna think it he.
Till he said, "I'm come back for to marry thee!"

O, sair did we greet, and muckle did we say!
We took but ae kiss, and we tore ourselves away!
I wish I were dead! but I'm no like to dee;
And why do I live to say "Wae's me!"?

I gang like a ghaist; and I carena to spin!
I darena think of Jemmy; for that wou'd be a sin!
But I'll do my best a gude wife to be;
For auld Robin Gray is kind unto me.

THOMAS CHATTERTON (1752-1770)

MYNSTRELLES SONGE

O! synge untoe mie roundelaie,
O! droppe the brynie teare wythe mee,
Daunce ne moe atte hallie daie,
Lycke a reynynge [1] ryver bee
    Mie love ys dedde,
    Gon to hys deathe-bedde,
    Al under the wyllowe tree.

[1] Running.

Blacke hys cryne [1] as the wyntere nyghte,
Whyte hys rode [2] as the summer snowe,
Rodde hys face as the mornynge lyghte,
Cale he lyes ynne the grave belowe;
    Mie love ys dedde,
      Gon to hys deathe-bedde,
    Al under the wyllowe tree.

Swote hys tyngue as the throstles note,
Quycke ynn daunce as thoughte canne bee,
Defte his taboure, codgelle stote,
O! hee lyes bie the wyllowe tree:
    Mie love ys dedde,
      Gonne to hys deathe-bedde,
    Alle underre the wyllowe tree.

Harke! the ravenne flappes hys wynge,
In the briered delle belowe;
Harke! the dethe-owle loud dothe synge,
To the nyghte-mares as heie goe;
    Mie love ys dedde,
      Gonne to hys deathe-bedde,
    Al under the wyllowe tree.

See! the whyte moone sheenes onne hie;
Whyteere ys mie true loves shroude;
Whyterre yanne the mornynge skie,
Whyterre yanne the evenynge cloude;
    Mie love ys dedde,
      Gon to hys deathe-bedde,
    Al under the wyllowe tree.

Heere, uponne mie true loves grave,
Schalle the baren fleurs be layde,
Nee one hallie Seyncte to save
Al the celness of a mayde.
    Mie love ys dedde,
      Gonne to hys death-bedde,
    Alle under the wyllowe tree.

[1] Hair.   [2] Complexion.

Wythe mie hondes I'lle dente the brieres
Round his hallie corse to gre,
Ouphante fairie, lyghte youre fyres,
Heere mie boddie stylle schalle bee.
   Mie love ys dedde,
   Gon to hys death-bedde,
   Al under the wyllowe tree.

Comme, wythe acorne-coppe & thorne,
Drayne mie hartys blodde awaie;
Lyfe & all yttes goode I scorne,
Daunce bie nete, or feaste by daie.
   Mie love ys dedde,
   Gon to hys death-bedde,
   Al under the wyllowe tree.

Waterre wytches, crownede wythe reytes,[1]
Bere mee to yer leathalle tyde.
I die; I comme; mie true love waytes.
Thos the damselle spake, and dyed.

GEORGE CRABBE (1754-1832)

From THE VILLAGE

The Village Life, and every care that reigns
O'er youthful peasants and declining swains;
What labour yields, and what, that labour past,
Age, in its hour of languor, finds at last;
What form the real picture of the poor,
Demand a song—the Muse can give no more.
  Fled are those times, when, in harmonious strains,
The rustic poet praised his native plains:
No shepherds now, in smooth alternate verse,
Their country's beauty or their nymphs' rehearse;
Yet still for these we frame the tender strain,
Still in our lays fond Corydons complain,
And shepherds' boys their amorous pains reveal,
The only pains, alas! they never feel.

[1] Water-flags.

On Mincio's banks, in Caesar's bounteous reign,
If Tityrus found the Golden Age again,
Must sleepy bards the flattering dream prolong,
Mechanic echoes of the Mantuan song?
From Truth and Nature shall we widely stray,
Where Virgil, not where Fancy, leads the way?
   Yes, thus the Muses sing of happy swains,
Because the Muses never knew their pains:
They boast their peasants' pipes; but peasants now
Resign their pipes and plod behind the plough;
And few, amid the rural-tribe, have time
To number syllables, and play with rhyme;
Save honest Duck, what son of verse could share
The poet's rapture, and the peasant's care?
Or the great labours of the field degrade,
With the new peril of a poorer trade?
   From this chief cause these idle praises spring,
That themes so easy few forbear to sing;
For no deep thought the trifling subjects ask;
To sing of shepherds is an easy task:
The happy youth assumes the common strain,
A nymph his mistress, and himself a swain;
With no sad scenes he clouds his tuneful prayer,
But all, to look like her, is painted fair.
   I grant indeed that fields and flocks have charms
For him that grazes or for him that farms;
But when amid such pleasing scenes I trace
The poor laborious natives of the place,
And see the mid-day sun, with fervid ray,
On their bare heads and dewy temples play;
While some, with feebler heads and fainter hearts,
Deplore their fortune, yet sustain their parts:
Then shall I dare these real ills to hide
In tinsel trappings of poetic pride?
   No; cast by Fortune on a frowning coast,
Which neither groves nor happy valleys boast;
Where other cares than those the Muse relates,
And other shepherds dwell with other mates;

By such examples taught, I paint the Cot,
As Truth will paint it, and as Bards will not:
Nor you, ye poor, of letter'd scorn complain,
To you the smoothest song is smooth in vain;
O'ercome by labour, and bow'd down by time,
Feel you the barren flattery of a rhyme?
Can poets soothe you, when you pine for bread,
By winding myrtles round your ruin'd shed?
Can their light tales your weighty griefs o'erpower,
Or glad with airy mirth the toilsome hour?
  Lo! where the heath, with withering brake grown o'er,
Lends the light turf that warms the neighbouring poor;
From thence a length of burning sand appears,
Where the thin harvest waves its wither'd ears;
Rank weeds, that every art and care defy,
Reign o'er the land, and rob the blighted rye:
There thistles stretch their prickly arms afar,
And to the ragged infant threaten war;
There poppies nodding, mock the hope of toil;
There the blue bugloss paints the sterile soil;
Hardy and high, above the slender sheaf,
The slimy mallow waves her silky leaf;
O'er the young shoot the charlock throws a shade,
And clasping tares cling round the sickly blade;
With mingled tints the rocky coasts abound,
And a sad splendour vainly shines around.
So looks the nymph whom wretched arts adorn.
Betray'd by man, then left for man to scorn;
Whose cheek in vain assumes the mimic rose,
While her sad eyes the troubled breast disclose;
Whose outward splendour is but folly's dress,
Exposing most, when most it gilds distress.
  Here joyless roam a wild amphibious race,
With sullen wo display'd in every face;
Who, far from civil arts and social fly,
And scowl at strangers with suspicious eye.
  Here too the lawless merchant of the main
Draws from his plough th' intoxicated swain;

Want only claim'd the labour of the day,
But vice now steals his nightly rest away.
　　Where are the swains, who, daily labour done,
With rural games play'd down the setting sun ;
Who struck with matchless force the bounding ball,
Or made the pond'rous quoit obliquely fall ;
While some huge Ajax, terrible and strong,
Engaged some artful stripling of the throng,
And fell beneath him, foil'd, while far around
Hoarse triumph rose, and rocks return'd the sound ?
Where now are these ?—Beneath yon cliff they stand,
To show the freighted pinnace where to land ;
To load the ready steed with guilty haste,
To fly in terror o'er the pathless waste,
Or, when detected, in their straggling course,
To foil their foes by cunning or by force ;
Or, yielding part (which equal knaves demand),
To gain a lawless passport through the land.
　　Here, wand'ring long, amid these frowning fields,
I sought the simple life that Nature yields ;
Rapine and Wrong and Fear usurp'd her place,
And a bold, artful, surly, savage race ;
Who, only skill'd to take the finny tribe,
The yearly dinner, or septennial bribe,
Wait on the shore, and, as the waves run high,
On the tost vessel bend their eager eye,
Which to their coast directs its vent'rous way ;
Theirs, or the ocean's, miserable prey.
　　As on their neighbouring beach yon swallows stand,
And wait for favouring winds to leave the land ;
While still for flight the ready wing is spread :
So waited I the favouring hour, and fled ;
Fled from these shores where guilt and famine reign,
And cried, Ah ! hapless they who still remain ;
Who still remain to hear the ocean roar,
Whose greedy waves devour the lessening shore ;
Till some fierce tide, with more imperious sway,
Sweeps the low hut and all it holds away ;

When the sad tenant weeps from door to door,
And begs a poor protection from the poor!
 But these are scenes where Nature's niggard hand
Gave a spare portion to the famish'd land;
Hers is the fault, if here mankind complain
Of fruitless toil and labour spent in vain;
But yet in other scenes more fair in view,
Where Plenty smiles—alas! she smiles for few—
And those who taste not, yet behold her store,
Are as the slaves that dig the golden ore,—
The wealth around them makes them doubly poor.
 Or will you deem them amply paid in health,
Labour's fair child, that languishes with wealth?
Go then! and see them rising with the sun,
Through a long course of daily toil to run;
See them beneath the dog-star's raging heat,
When the knees tremble and the temples beat;
Behold them, leaning on their scythes, look o'er
The labour past, and toils to come explore;
See them alternate suns and showers engage,
And hoard up aches and anguish for their age;
Through fens and marshy moors their steps pursue,
When their warm pores imbibe the evening dew;
Then own that labour may as fatal be
To these thy slaves, as thine excess to thee.
 Amid this tribe too oft a manly pride
Strives in strong toil the fainting heart to hide;
There may you see the youth of slender frame
Contend with weakness, weariness, and shame;
Yet, urged along, and proudly loth to yield,
He strives to join his fellows of the field.
Till long-contending nature droops at last,
Declining health rejects his poor repast,
His cheerless spouse the coming danger sees,
And mutual murmurs urge the slow disease.
 Yet grant them health, 'tis not for us to tell,
Though the head droops not, that the heart is well;
Or will you praise that homely, healthy fare,
Plenteous and plain, that happy peasants share!

Oh! trifle not with wants you cannot feel,
Nor mock the misery of a stinted meal;
Homely, not wholesome, plain, not plenteous, such
As you who praise would never deign to touch.
   Ye gentle souls, who dream of rural ease,
Whom the smooth stream and smoother sonnet please;
Go! if the peaceful cot your praises share,
Go look within, and ask if peace be there;
If peace be his—that drooping weary sire,
Or theirs, that offspring round their feeble fire;
Or hers, that matron pale, whose trembling hand
Turns on the wretched hearth th' expiring brand! . . .
   Thus groan the old, till, by disease oppress'd,
They taste a final wo, and then they rest.
   Theirs is yon house that holds the parish-poor,
Whose walls of mud scarce bear the broken door;
There, where the putrid vapours, flagging, play,
And the dull wheel hums doleful through the day;—
There children dwell who know no parents' care;
Parents, who know no children's love, dwell there!
Heartbroken matrons on their joyless bed,
Forsaken wives, and mothers never wed;
Dejected widows with unheeded tears,
And crippled age with more than childhood fears;
The lame, the blind, and, far the happiest they!
The moping idiot and the madman gay.
Here too the sick their final doom receive,
Here brought, amid the scenes of grief, to grieve,
Where the loud groans from some sad chamber
    flow,
Mix'd with the clamours of the crowd below;
Here, sorrowing, they each kindred sorrow scan,
And the cold charities of man to man:
Whose laws indeed for ruin'd age provide,
And strong compulsion plucks the scrap from pride;
But still that scrap is bought with many a sigh,
And pride embitters what it can't deny.
   Say ye, oppress'd by some fantastic woes,
Some jarring nerve that baffles your repose;

Who press the downy couch, while slaves advance
With timid eye, to read the distant glance ;
Who with sad prayers the weary doctor tease,
To name the nameless ever-new disease ;
Who with mock patience dire complaints endure,
Which real pain and that alone can cure ;
How would ye bear in real pain to lie,
Despised, neglected, left alone to die ?
How would ye bear to draw your latest breath,
Where all that's wretched paves the way for death ?
   Such is that room which one rude beam divides,
And naked rafters form the sloping sides ;
Where the vile bands that bind the thatch are seen,
And lath and mud are all that lie between ;
Save one dull pane, that, coarsely patch'd, gives way
To the rude tempest, yet excludes the day :
Here, on a matted flock, with dust o'erspread,
The drooping wretch reclines his languid head ;
For him no hand the cordial cup applies,
Or wipes the tear that stagnates in his eyes ;
No friends with soft discourse his pain beguile,
Or promise hope till sickness wears a smile.
   But soon a loud and hasty summons calls,
Shakes the thin roof, and echoes round the walls ;
Anon, a figure enters, quaintly neat,
All pride and business, bustle and conceit ;
With looks unalter'd by these scenes of wo,
With speed that, entering, speaks his haste to go,
He bids the gazing throng around him fly,
And carries fate and physic in his eye :
A potent quack, long versed in human ills,
Who first insults the victim whom he kills ;
Whose murd'rous hand a drowsy Bench protect,
And whose most tender mercy is neglect.
   Paid by the parish for attendance here,
He wears contempt upon his sapient sneer ;
In haste he seeks the bed where Misery lies,
Impatience mark'd in his averted eyes ;

And, some habitual queries hurried o'er,
Without reply, he rushes on the door :
His drooping patient, long inured to pain,
And long unheeded, knows remonstrance vain ;
He ceases now the feeble help to crave
Of man ; and silent sinks into the grave.
   But ere his death some pious doubts arise,
Some simple fears, which " bold bad " men despise ;
Fain would he ask the parish-priest to prove
His title certain to the joys above :
For this he sends the murmuring nurse, who calls
The holy stranger to these dismal walls :
And doth not he, the pious man, appear,
He, " passing rich with forty pounds a year " ?
Ah ! no ; a shepherd of a different stock,
And far unlike him, feeds this little flock :
A jovial youth, who thinks his Sunday's task
As much as God or man can fairly ask ;
The rest he gives to loves and labours light,
To fields the morning, and to feasts the night ;
None better skill'd the noisy pack to guide,
To urge their chase, to cheer them or to chide ;
A sportsman keen, he shoots through half the day,
And, skill'd at whist, devotes the night to play :
Then, while such honours bloom around his head,
Shall he sit sadly by the sick man's bed,
To raise the hope he feels not, or with zeal
To combat fears that e'en the pious feel ?
   Now once again the gloomy scene explore,
Less gloomy now ; the bitter hour is o'er,
The man of many sorrows sighs no more.—
Up yonder hill, behold how sadly slow
The bier moves winding from the vale below ;
There lie the happy dead, from trouble free,
And the glad parish pays the frugal fee :
No more, O Death ! thy victim starts to hear
Churchwarden stern, or kingly overseer ;
No more the farmer claims his humble bow,
Thou art his lord, the best of tyrants thou !

Now to the church behold the mourners come,
Sedately torpid and devoutly dumb;
The village children now their games suspend,
To see the bier that bears their ancient friend;
For he was one in all their idle sport,
And like a monarch ruled their little court
The pliant bow he form'd, the flying ball,
The bat, the wicket, were his labours all;
Him now they follow to his grave, and stand
Silent and sad, and gazing, hand in hand;
While bending low, their eager eyes explore
The mingled relics of the parish poor:
The bell tolls late, the moping owl flies round,
Fear marks the flight and magnifies the sound;
The busy priest, detain'd by weightier care,
Defers his duty till the day of prayer;
And, waiting long, the crowd retire distress'd,
To think a poor man's bones should lie unbless'd.

ROBERT BURNS (1759-1796)

TAM O' SHANTER

When chapman billies leave the street,
And drouthy neibors neibors meet,
As market-days are wearing late,
An' folk begin to tak the gate;
While we sit bousing at the nappy,
An' getting fou and unco happy,
We think na on the lang Scots miles,
The mosses, waters, slaps, and styles,
That lie between us and our hame,
Where sits our sulky sullen dame,
Gathering her brows like gathering storm,
Nursing her wrath to keep it warm.
 This truth fand honest Tam o' Shanter,
As he frae Ayr ae night did canter—
(Auld Ayr, wham ne'er a town surpasses
For honest men and bonnie lasses).

O Tam! hadst thou but been sae wise
As ta'en thy ain wife Kate's advice!
She tauld thee weel thou was a skellum,
A bletherin', blusterin', drunken blellum ;
That frae November till October,
Ae market-day thou was na sober ;
That ilka melder wi' the miller
Thou sat as lang as thou had siller ;
That every naig was ca'd a shoe on,
The smith and thee gat roarin' fou on ;
That at the Lord's house, even on Sunday,
Thou drank wi' Kirkton Jean till Monday.
She prophesied that, late or soon,
Thou would be found deep drown'd 'n Doon ;
Or catch'd wi' warlocks in the mirk
By Alloway's auld haunted kirk.
 Ah, gentle dames! it gars me greet
To think how mony counsels sweet,
How mony lengthen'd sage advices,
The husband frae the wife despises!
 But to our tale : Ae market night,
Tam had got planted unco right,
Fast by an ingle, bleezing finely,
Wi' reaming swats, that drank divinely ;
And at his elbow, Souter Johnny,
His ancient, trusty, drouthy crony ;
Tam lo'ed him like a very brither ;
They had been fou for weeks thegither.
The night drave on wi' sangs and clatter,
And aye the ale was growing better :
The landlady and Tam grew gracious,
Wi' favours secret, sweet, and precious ;
The souter tauld his queerest stories ;
The landlord's laugh was ready chorus :
The storm without might rair and rustle,
Tam did na mind the storm a whistle.
 Care, mad to see man sae happy,
E'en drown'd himsel amang the nappy.
As bees flee hame wi' lades o' treasure,

The minutes wing'd their way wi' pleasure;
Kings may be blest, but Tam was glorious,
O'er a' the ills o' life victorious!
  But pleasures are like poppies spread—
You seize the flow'r, its bloom is shed;
Or like the snow falls in the river—
A moment white, then melts for ever;
Or like the borealis race,
That flit ere you can point their place;
Or like the rainbow's lovely form
Evanishing amid the storm.
Nae man can tether time nor tide;
The hour approaches Tam maun ride;
That hour, o' night's black arch the key-stane,
That dreary hour, he mounts his beast in;
And sic a night he taks the road in,
As ne'er poor sinner was abroad in.
  The wind blew as 'twad blawn its last;
The rattling show'rs rose on the blast;
The speedy gleams the darkness swallow'd;
Loud, deep and lang, the thunder bellow'd:
That night, a child might understand,
The Deil had business on his hand.
  Weel mounted on his grey mare, Meg,
A better never lifted leg,
Tam skelpit on thro' dub and mire,
Despising wind, and rain, and fire;
Whiles holding fast his gude blue bonnet;
Whiles crooning o'er some auld Scots sonnet;
Whiles glow'ring round wi' prudent cares,
Lest bogles catch him unawares.
Kirk-Alloway was drawing nigh,
Whare ghaists and houlets nightly cry.
  By this time he was cross the ford,
Where in the snaw the chapman smoor'd;
And past the birks and meikle stane,
Where drunken Charlie brak's neck-bane;
And thro' the whins, and by the cairn,
Where hunters fand the murder'd bairn;

And near the thorn, aboon the well,
Where Mungo's mither hang'd hersel.
Before him Doon pours all his floods ;
The doubling storm roars thro' the woods ;
The lightnings flash from pole to pole ;
Near and more near the thunders roll :
When, glimmering thro' the groaning trees,
Kirk-Alloway seem'd in a bleeze ;
Thro' ilka bore the beams were glancing ;
And loud resounded mirth and dancing.
   Inspiring bold John Barleycorn !
What dangers thou canst make us scorn !
Wi' tippenny, we fear nae evil ;
Wi' usquebae, we'll face the devil !
The swats sae ream'd in Tammie's noddle,
Fair play, he car'd na deils a boddle !
But Maggie stood right sair astonish'd,
Till, by the heel and hand admonish'd,
She ventur'd forward on the light ;
And, vow ! Tam saw an unco sight !
Warlocks and witches in a dance !
Nae cotillon brent new frae France,
But hornpipes, jigs, strathspeys, and reels,
Put life and mettle in their heels.
A winnock-bunker in the east,
There sat auld Nick, in shape o' beast—
A touzie tyke, black, grim, and large !
To gie them music was his charge :
He screw'd the pipes and gart them skirl.
Till roof and rafters a' did dirl.
Coffins stood round like open presses,
That shaw'd the dead in their last dresses ;
And by some devilish cantraip sleight
Each in its cauld hand held a light,
By which heroic Tam was able
To note upon the haly table
A murderer's banes in gibbet-airns ;
Twa span-lang, wee, unchristen'd bairns ;
A thief new-cutted frae the rape—

Wi' his last gasp his bab did gape ;
Five tomahawks, wi' blude red rusted ;
Five scymitars, wi' murder crusted ;
A garter, which a babe had strangled ;
A knife, a father's throat had mangled,
Whom his ain son o' life bereft—
The gray hairs yet stack to the heft ;
Wi' mair of horrible and awfu',
Which even to name wad be unlawfu'.
　　As Tammie glowr'd, amaz'd, and curious,
The mirth and fun grew fast and furious :
The piper loud and louder blew ;
The dancers quick and quicker flew ;
They reel'd, they set, they cross'd, they cleekit,
Yill ilka carlin swat and reekit,
And coost her duddies to the wark,
And linkit at it in her sark ! . . .
　　But here my muse her wing maun cour ;
Sic flights are far beyond her pow'r—
To sing how Nannie lap and flang,
(A souple jade she was, and strang) ;
And how Tam stood, like ane bewitch'd,
And thought his very een enrich'd ;
Even Satan glowr'd, and fidg'd fu' fain,
And hotch'd and blew wi' might and main :
Till first ae caper, syne anither,
Tam tint his reason a' thegither,
And roars out " Weel done, Cutty-sark ! "
And in an instant all was dark !
And scarcely had he Maggie rallied,
When out the hellish legion sallied.
　　As bees bizz out wi' angry fyke
When plundering herds assail their byke,
As open pussie's mortal foes
When pop ! she starts before their nose,
As eager runs the market-crowd,
When " Catch the thief ! " resounds aloud.
So Maggie runs ; the witches follow,
Wi' mony an eldritch skriech and hollow.

Ah, Tam! ah, Tam! thou'll get thy fairin'!
In hell they'll roast thee like a herrin'!
In vain thy Kate awaits thy comin'!
Kate soon will be a woefu' woman!
Now do thy speedy utmost, Meg,
And win the key-stane o' the brig:
There at them thou thy tail may toss,
A running stream they darena cross.
But ere the key-stane she could make,
The fient a tail she had to shake!
For Nannie, far before the rest,
Hard upon noble Maggie prest,
And flew at Tam wi' furious ettle;
But little wist she Maggie's mettle!
Ae spring brought off her master hale,
But left behind her ain gray tail:
The carlin claught her by the rump,
And left poor Maggie scarce a stump.

 Now, wha this tale o' truth shall read,
Each man and mother's son, take heed;
Whene'er to drink you are inclin'd,
Or cutty-sarks rin in your mind,
Think! ye may buy the joys o'er dear;
Remember Tam o' Shanter's mare.

ADDRESS TO THE DEIL

O THOU! whatever title suit thee,
Auld Hornie, Satan, Nick, or Clootie,
Wha in yon cavern grim an' sootie,
   Clos'd under hatches,
Spairges about the brunstane cootie,
   To scaud poor wretches!

Hear me, auld Hangie, for a wee,
An' let poor damnèd bodies be;
I'm sure sma' pleasure it can gie,
   Ev'n to a deil,
To skelp an' scaud poor dogs like me,
   An' hear us squeal!

Great is thy pow'r, an' great thy fame;
Far kenn'd an' noted is thy name;
An', tho' yon lowin heugh's thy hame,
  Thou travels far;
An' faith! thou's neither lag nor lame,
  Nor blate nor scaur.

Whyles rangin' like a roarin' lion
For prey, a' holes an' corners tryin';
Whyles on the strong-wing'd tempest flyin',
  Tirlin' the kirks;
Whyles, in the human bosom pryin',
  Unseen thou lurks.

I've heard my reverend grannie say,
In lanely glens ye like to stray;
Or, where auld ruin'd castles gray
  Nod to the moon,
Ye fright the nightly wand'rer's way,
  Wi' eldritch croon.

When twilight did my grannie summon
To say her pray'rs, douce, honest woman!
Aft yont the dyke she's heard you bummin',
  Wi' eerie drone;
Or, rustlin', thro' the boortrees comin',
  Wi' heavy groan.

Ae dreary windy winter night
The stars shot down wi' sklentin' light,
Wi' you mysel I gat a fright
  Ayont the lough;
Ye like a rash-buss stood in sight
  Wi' waving sough.

The cudgel in my nieve did shake,
Each bristled hair stood like a stake,
When wi' an eldritch stoor ' quaick, quaick,"
  Amang the springs,
Awa ye squatter'd like a drake
  On whistlin' wings.

Let warlocks grim an' wither'd hags
Tell how wi' you on ragweed nags
They skim the muirs, an' dizzy crags
  Wi' wicked speed ;
And in kirk-yards renew their leagues
  Owre howkit dead.

Thence country wives, wi' toil an' pain,
May plunge an' plunge the kirn in vain ;
For oh ! the yellow treasure's taen
  By witchin' skill ;
An' dawtit twal-pint Hawkie's gane
  As yell's the bill.

Thence mystic knots mak great abuse
On young guidmen, fond, keen, an' crouse ;
When the best wark-lume i' the house,
  By cantrip wit,
Is instant made no worth a louse,
  Just at the bit.

When thowes dissolve the snawy hoord,
An' float the jinglin' icy-boord,
Then water-kelpies haunt the foord,
  By your direction,
An' 'nighted trav'llers are allur'd
  To their destruction.

An' aft your moss-traversing spunkies
Decoy the wight that late an' drunk is:
The bleezin, curst, mischievous monkies
    Delude his eyes,
Till in some miry slough he sunk is,
    Ne'er mair to rise.

When masons' mystic word an' grip
In storms an' tempests raise you up,
Some cock or cat your rage maun stop,
    Or, stange to tell!
The youngest brither ye wad whip
    Aff straught to hell.

Lang syne, in Eden's bonnie yard,
When youthfu' lovers first were pair'd,
And all the soul of love they shar'd,
    The raptur'd hour,
Sweet on the fragrant flow'ry swaird,
    In shady bow'r;

Then you, ye auld snick-drawing dog!
Ye cam to Paradise incog.
An' play'd on man a cursed brogue,
    (Black be you fa!)
An' gied the infant warld a shog,
    'Maist ruin'd a'.

D'ye mind that day, when in a bizz,
Wi' reekit duds, an' reestit gizz,
Ye did present your smoutie phiz
    'Mang better folk,
An' sklented on the man of Uz
    Your spitefu' joke?

An' how ye gat him i' your thrall,
An' brak him out o' house an' hal'.
While scabs an' blotches did him gall
    Wi' bitter claw,
An' lows'd his ill-tongu'd wicked scawl,
    Was warst ava?

But a' your doings to rehearse,
Your wily snares an' fechtin' fierce,
Sin' that day Michael did you pierce,
    Down to this time,
Wad ding a' Lallan tongue, or Erse,
    In prose or rhyme.

An' now, auld Cloots, I ken ye're thinkin',
A certain Bardie's rantin', drinkin',
Some luckless hour will send him linkin',
    To your black pit;
But faith! he'll turn a corner jinkin',
    An' cheat you yet.

But fare you weel, auld Nickie-ben!
O wad ye tak a thought an' men'!
Ye aiblins might—I dinna ken—
    Still hae a stake:
I'm wae to think upo' yon den,
    Ev'n for your sake!

ADDRESS TO THE UNCO GUID, OR THE RIGIDLY RIGHTEOUS

O YE wha are sae guid yoursel,
    Sae pious and sae holy,
Ye've nought to do but mark and tell
    Your neibour's fauts and folly!
Whase life is like a well-gaun mill,
    Supplied wi' store o' water:
The heaped happer's ebbing still,
    And still the clap plays clatter:

Hear me, ye venerable core,
  As counsel for poor mortals,
That frequent pass douce Wisdom's door,
  For glaikit Folly's portals;
I, for their thoughtless careless sakes,
  Would here propone defences,—
Their donsie tricks, their black mistakes,
  Their failings and mischances.

Ye see your state wi' theirs compar'd,
  And shudder at the niffer;
But cast a moment's fair regard—
  What maks the mighty differ?
Discount what scant occasion gave,
  That purity ye pride in,
And (what's aft mair than a' the lave)
  Your better art o' hidin'. . . .

Then gently scan your brother man,
  Still gentler sister woman;
Tho' they may gang a kennin wrang,
  To step aside is human.
One point must still be greatly dark,
  The moving why they do it;
And just as lamely can ye mark
  How far perhaps they rue it.

Who made the heart, 'tis He alone
  Decidedly can try us;
He knows each chord, its various tone,
  Each spring, its various bias.
Then at the balance let's be mute,
  We never can adjust it;
What's done we partly may compute,
  But know not what's resisted.

FOR A' THAT AND A' THAT

Is there, for honest poverty,
  That hangs his head, and a' that?
The coward-slave, we pass him by,
  We dare be poor for a' that!
    For a' that, and a' that,
      Our toils obscure, and a' that;
    The rank is but the guinea stamp;
      The man's the gowd for a' that.

What tho' on hamely fare we dine,
  Wear hodden-gray, and a' that;
Gie fools their silks, and knaves their wine,
  A man's a man for a' that.
    For a' that, and a' that,
      Their tinsel show, and a' that;
    The honest man, tho' e'er sae poor,
      Is King o' men for a' that.

Ye see yon birkie, ca'd a lord,
  Wha struts, and stares, and a' that;
Tho' hundreds worship at his word,
  He's but a coof for a' that:
    For a' that, and a' that,
      His riband, star, and a' that,
    The man of independent mind,
      He looks and laughs and a' that.

A prince can mak a belted knight,
  A marquis, duke, and a' that;
But an honest man's aboon his might,
  Guid faith he mauna fa' that!
    For a' that, and a' that,
      Their dignities, and a' that,
    The pith o' sense, and pride o' worth,
      Are higher rank than a' that.

Then let us pray that come it may,
  As come it will for a' that;
That sense and worth, o'er a' the earth,
  May bear the gree, and a' that.
    For a' that and a' that,
      It's coming yet, for a' that,
    That man to man the warld o'er
      Shall brothers be for a' that.

TO A MOUSE, ON TURNING HER UP IN HER NEST WITH THE PLOUGH, NOVEMBER, 1785

Wee, sleekit, cow'rin, tim'rous beastie,
O what a panic's in thy breastie!
Thou need na start awa sae hasty,
            Wi' bickering brattle!
I wad be laith to rin an' chase thee
            Wi' murd'ring pattle!

I'm truly sorry man's dominion
Has broken Nature's social union,
An' justifies that ill opinion
            Which makes thee startle
At me, thy poor earth-born companion,
            An' fellow-mortal!

I doubt na, whiles, but thou may thieve;
What then? poor beastie, thou maun live!
A daimen-icker in a thrave
            'S a sma' request:
I'll get a blessin' wi' the lave,
            And never miss't!

Thy wee bit housie, too, in ruin!
Its silly wa's the win's are strewin'!
An' naething, now, to big a new ane,
            O' foggage green!
An' bleak December's winds ensuin',
            Baith snell an' keen!

Thou saw the fields laid bare and waste,
An' weary winter comin' fast,
An' cozie here, beneath the blast,
        Thou thought to dwell,
Till crash! the cruel coulter past
        Out-thro' thy cell.

That wee bit heap o' leaves an' stibble
Has cost thee mony a weary nibble!
Now thou's turn'd out, for a' thy trouble,
        But house or hald,
To thole the winter's sleety dribble,
        An' cranreuch cauld!

But, Mousie, thou art no thy lane,
In proving foresight may be vain:
The best laid schemes o' mice an' men
        Gang oft a-gley,
An' lea'e us nought but grief an' pain
        For promis'd joy.

Still thou art blest compar'd wi' me!
The present only toucheth thee:
But oh! I backward cast my e'e
        On prospects drear!
An' forward tho' I canna see,
        I guess an' fear!

A WINTER NIGHT

When biting Boreas, fell and dour
Sharp shivers thro' the leafless bow'r;
When Phœbus gies a short-liv'd glow'r
        Far south the lift,
Dim-darkening thro' the flaky show'r
        Or whirling drift;

Ae night the storm the steeples rocked,
Poor Labour sweet in sleep was rocked
While burns wi' snawy wreaths up-choked,
    Wild-eddying swirl,
Or, thro, the mining outlet blocked,
    Down headlong hurl:

Listening the doors and winnocks rattle,
I thought me on the ourie cattle,
Or silly sheep that bide this brattle
    O' winter war,
An thro' the drift deep-lairing spratlle
    Beneath a scaur.

Ilk happin' bird—wee, helpless thing!
That in the merry months o' spring
Delighted me to hear thee sing,
    What comes o' thee?
Whare wilt thou cow'r thy chittering wing
    An' close thy ee?

Ev'n you on murd'ring errands toil'd,
Lone from your savage homes exil'd,
The blood-stain'd roost an' sheep-cot spoil'd
    My heart forgets,
While pitiless the tempest wild
    Sore on you beats.

JOHN BARLEYCORN

A BALLAD

There was three Kings into the east,
    Three Kings both great and high,
And they hae sworn a solemn oath
    John Barleycorn should die.

They took a plough and plough'd him down,
    Put clods upon his head,
And they hae sworn a solemn oath
    John Barleycorn was dead.

But the cheerfu' Spring came kindly on,
    And show'rs began to fall;
John Barleycorn got up again,
    And sore surpris'd them all.

The sultry suns of Summer came,
    And he grew thick and strong,
His head weel arm'd wi' pointed spears,
    That no one should him wrong.

The sober Autumn enter'd mild,
    When he grew wan and pale;
His bending joints and drooping head
    Show'd he began to fail.

His colour sicken'd more and more,
    He faded into age;
And then his enemies began
    To shew their deadly rage.

They've ta'en a weapon, long and sharp,
    And cut him by the knee;
Then tied him fast upon a cart,
    Like a rogue for forgerie,

They laid him down upon his back,
    And cudgell'd him full sore;
They hung him up before the storm,
    And turn'd him o'er and o'er.

They fillèd up a darksome pit
    With water to the brim,
They heavèd in John Barleycorn,
    There let him sink or swim.

They laid him out upon the floor,
    To work him farther woe,
And still, as signs of life appear'd,
    They toss'd him to and fro.

They wasted, o'er a scorching flame
  The marrow of his bones ;
But a miller us'd him worst of all,
  For he crush'd him between two stones.

And they hae ta'en his very heart's blood,
  And drank it round and round ;
And still the more and more they drank,
  Their joy did more abound.

John Barleycorn was a hero bold,
  Of noble enterprise,
For if you do but taste his blood,
  'Twill make your courage rise ;

'Twill make a man forget his woe ;
  'Twill heighten all his joy ;
'Twill make the widow's heart to sing,
  Tho' the tear were in her eye.

Then let us toast John Barleycorn,
  Each man a glass in hand ;
And may his great posterity
  Ne'er fail in old Scotland !

LAST MAY A BRAW WOOER

Last May a braw wooer cam down the lang glen,
  And sair wi' his love he did deave me :
I said there was naething I hated like men—
  The deuce gae wi'm to believe me, believe me,
  The deuce gae wi'm to believe me.

He spak o' the darts in my bonnie black een,
  And vow'd for my love he was dying ;
I said he might die when he liked for Jean :
  The Lord forgie me for lying, for lying,
  The Lord forgie me for lying !

A weel-stockèd mailen, himsel' for the laird,
  And marriage aff-hand, were his proffers :
I never loot on that I kend it, or car'd ;
  But thought I might hae waur offers, waur offers,
  But thought I might hae waur offers.

But what wad ye think ? in a fortnight or less,
  The deil tak his taste to gae near her !
He up the lang loan to my black cousin Bess,
  Guess ye how, the jad ! I could bear her, could bear her,
  Guess ye how, the jad ! I could bear her.

But a' the niest week as I fretted wi' care,
  I gaed to the tryst o' Dalgarnock ;
And wha but my fine fickle lover was there ?
  I glowr'd as I'd seen a warlock, a warlock,
  I glowr'd as I'd seen a warlock.

But owre my left shouther I gae him a blink,
  Lest neebors might say I was saucy ;
My wooer he caper'd as he'd been in drink,
  And vow'd I was his dear lassie, dear lassie,
  And vow'd I was his dear lassie.

I spier'd for my cousin fu' couthy and sweet,
  Gin she had recover'd her hearin',
And how her new shoon fit her auld shachl't feet—
  But, heavens ! how he fell a swearin', a swearin',
  But, heavens ! how he fell a swearin'.

He beggèd for Gudesake I wad be his wife
  Or else I wad kill him wi' sorrow :
So e'en to preserve the poor body in life,
  I think I maun wed him to-morrow, to-morrow,
  I think I maun wed him to-morrow.

ROBERT BRUCE'S ADDRESS TO HIS ARMY BEFORE THE BATTLE OF BANNOCKBURN

Scots wha hae with Wallace bled,
Scots wham Bruce has aften led,
Welcome to your gory bed,
 Or to victorie.

Now's the day, and now's the hour;
See the front o' battle lour!
See approach proud Edward's power—
 Chains and slaverie!

Wha will be a traitor knave?
Wha can fill a coward's grave?
Wha sae base as be a slave?
 Let him turn and flee!

Wha for Scotland's King and law
Freedom's sword will strongly draw,
Freeman stand, or freeman fa'?
 Let him follow me!

By oppression's woes and pains!
By your sons in servile chains!
We will drain our dearest veins,
 But they shall be free!

Lay the proud usurpers low!
Tyrants fall in every foe!
Liberty's in every blow!
 Let us do or die!

IT WAS A' FOR OUR RIGHTFU' KING

It was a' for our rightfu' King,
  We left fair Scotland's strand;
It was a' for our rightfu' King,
  We e'er saw Irish land,
      My dear,
  We e'er saw Irish land.

Now a' is done that men can do,
  And a' is done in vain;
My love and native land farewell,
  For I maun cross the main,
      My dear,
  For I maun cross the main.

He turn'd him right and round about
  Upon the Irish shore;
And gae his bridle-reins a shake,
  With adieu for evermore,
      My dear,
  Adieu for evermore.

The sodger from the wars returns,
  The sailor frae the main;
But I hae parted frae my love,
  Never to meet again,
      My dear,
  Never to meet again.

When day is gane, and night is come,
  And a' folk boune to sleep,
I think on him that's far awa',
  The lee-lang night, and weep,
      My dear,
  The lee-lang night, and weep.

AULD LANG SYNE

Should auld acquaintance be forgot,
    And never brought to min'?
Should auld acquaintance be forgot
    And auld lang syne?

    For auld lang syne, my dear,
        For auld lang syne,
    We'll tak a cup o' kindness yet,
        For auld lang syne.

We twa hae run about the braes,
    And pu'd the gowans fine.
But we've wander'd mony a weary foot
    Sin' auld lang syne.

We twa hae paidled i' the burn,
    From morning sun till dine
But seas between us braid hae roar'd
    Sin' auld lang syne.

And there's a hand, my trusty fiere,
    And gie's a hand of thine,
And we'll tak a right guid-willie waught,
    For auld lang syne.

And surely ye'll be your pint-stowp,
    And surely I'll be mine;
And we'll tak a cup o' kindness yet,
    For auld lang syne.

WHEN I SLEEP I DREAM

Whan I sleep I dream,
    Whan I wauk I'm eerie,
Sleep I canna get,
    For thinkin' o' my dearie.

Lanely night comes on,
  A' the house are sleeping;
I think on the bonnie lad
  That has my heart a keeping.

Lanely night comes on,
  A' the house are sleeping,
I think on my bonnie lad,
  An' I bleer my een wi' greetin'!
    Aye waukin O, waukin aye and wearie,
    Sleep I canna get for thinkin' o' my dearie.

BONNIE DOON

Ye flowery banks o' bonnie Doon,
  How can ye blume sae fair?
How can ye chant, ye little birds,
  And I sae fu' o' care?

Thou'll break my heart, thou bonnie bird,
  That sings upon the bough,
Thou minds me o' the happy days,
  When my fause luve was true.

Thou'll break my heart, thou bonnie bird,
  That sings beside thy mate;
For sae I sat, and sae I sang,
  And wist na o' my fate.

Aft hae I rov'd by bonnie Doon
  To see the wood-bine twine,
And ilka bird sang o' its luve,
  And sae did I o' mine.

Wi' lightsome heart I pu'd a rose
  Frae aff its thorny tree;
And my fause lover staw my rose
  But left the thorn wi' me.

MY LOVE IS LIKE A RED RED ROSE

My love is like a red red rose
 That's newly sprung in June:
My love is like the melodie
 That's sweetly play'd in tune.

So fair art thou, my bonnie lass,
 So deep in love am I:
And I will love thee still, my dear,
 Till a' the seas gang dry.

Till a' the seas gang dry, my dear,
 And the rocks melt wi' the sun:
And I will love thee still, my dear,
 While the sands o' life shall run.

And fare thee weel, my only love,
 And fare thee weel awhile!
And I will come again, my love,
 Tho' it were ten thousand mile.

O, WERT THOU IN THE CAULD BLAST

O, wert thou in the cauld blast,
 On yonder lea, on yonder lea,
My plaidie to the angry airt,
 I'd shelter thee, I'd shelter thee.
Or did misfortune's bitter storms
 Around thee blaw, around thee blaw,
Thy bield should be my bosom,
 To share it a', to share it a'.

Or were I in the wildest waste,
 Sae black and bare, sae black and bare,
The desert were a paradise,
 If thou wert there, if thou wert there.

Or were I monarch o' the globe,
  Wi' thee to reign, wi' thee to reign,
The brightest jewel in my crown
  Wad be my queen, wad be my queen.

FAREWELL TO NANCY

Ae fond kiss, and then we sever!
Ae fareweel, alas, for ever!
Deep in heart-wrung tears I'll pledge thee,
Warring sighs and groans I'll wage thee.

Who shall say that Fortune grieves him
While the star of hope she leaves him?
Me, nae cheerfu' twinkle lights me
Dark despair around benights me.

I'll ne'er blame my partial fancy,
Naething could resist my Nancy,
But to see her was to love her,
Love but her and love for ever.

Had we never loved sae kindly,
Had we never loved sae blindly,
Never met—or never parted,
We had ne'er been broken-hearted.

Fare thee weel, thou first and fairest!
Fare thee weel, thou best and dearest!
Thine be ilka joy and treasure,
Peace, enjoyment, love and pleasure.

Ae fond kiss, and then we sever!
Ae fareweel, alas, for ever!
Deep in heart-wrung tears I'll pledge thee,
Warring sighs and groans I'll wage thee.

WILLIAM BLAKE (1757-1827)
TO THE EVENING STAR

Thou fair-hair'd angel of the evening,
Now, whilst the sun rests on the mountains, light
Thy bright torch of love; thy radiant crown
Put on, and smile upon our evening bed!
Smile on our loves, and while thou drawest the
Blue curtains of the sky, scatter thy silver dew
On every flower that shuts its sweet eyes
In timely sleep. Let thy west wind sleep on
The lake; speak silence with thy glimmering eyes,
And wash the dusk with silver. Soon, full soon,
Dost thou withdraw; then the wolf rages wide,
And the lion glares thro' the dun forest:
The fleeces of our flocks are cover'd with
Thy sacred dew: protect them with thine influence.

INTRODUCTION TO SONGS OF INNOCENCE

Piping down the valleys wild,
Piping songs of pleasant glee,
On a cloud I saw a child,
And he laughing said to me:

"Pipe a song about a Lamb!"
So I piped with merry cheer.
"Piper, pipe that song again";
So I piped: he wept to hear.

"Drop thy pipe, thy happy pipe;
Sing thy songs of happy cheer:"
So I sang the same again,
While he wept with joy to hear.

"Piper, sit thee down and write
In a book that all may read."
So he vanish'd from my sight,
And I pluck'd a hollow reed,

And I made a rural pen,
And I stain'd the water clear,
And I wrote my happy songs
Every child may joy to hear.

THE LAMB

Little Lamb, who made thee?
Dost thou know who made thee?
Gave thee life, and bid thee feed
By the stream and o'er the mead;
Gave thee clothing of delight,
Softest clothing, woolly, bright;
Gave thee such a tender voice,
Making all the vales rejoice?
Little Lamb, who made thee?
Dost thou know who made thee?

Little Lamb, I'll tell thee,
Little Lamb, I'll tell thee:
He is callèd by thy name,
For He calls Himself a Lamb.
He is meek, and He is mild;
He became a little child.
I a child, and thou a lamb,
We are callèd by His name.
Little Lamb, God bless thee!
Little Lamb, God bless thee!

NIGHT

The sun descending in the west,
The evening star does shine;
The birds are silent in their nest,
And I must seek for mine.
The moon, like a flower,
In heaven's high bower,
With silent delight
Sits and smiles on the night.

Farewell, green fields and happy groves,
Where flocks have took delight.
Where lambs have nibbled, silent moves
The feet of angels bright;
Unseen they pour blessing,
And joy without ceasing,
On each bud and blossom,
And each sleeping bosom.

They look in every thoughtless nest,
Where birds are cover'd warm;
They visit caves of every beast,
To keep them all from harm.
If they see any weeping
That should have been sleeping,
They pour sleep on their head,
And sit down by their bed.

When wolves and tigers howl for prey,
They pitying stand and weep;
Seeking to drive their thirst away,
And keep them from the sheep.
But if they rush dreadful,
The angels, most heedful,
Receive each mild spirit,
New worlds to inherit.

And there the lion's ruddy eyes
Shall flow with tears of gold,
And pitying the tender cries,
And walking round the fold,
Saying " Wrath, by His meekness,
And, by His health, sickness
Is driven away
From our immortal day.

" And now beside thee, bleating lamb,
I can lie down and sleep;
Or think on Him who bore thy name,
Graze after thee and weep.
For, wash'd in life's river,
My bright mane for ever
Shall shine like the gold
As I guard o'er the fold."

THE TIGER

Tiger! Tiger! burning bright
In the forests of the night,
What immortal hand or eye
Could frame thy fearful symmetry?

In what distant deeps or skies
Burnt the fire of thine eyes?
On what wings dare he aspire?
What the hand dare seize the fire?

And what shoulder, and what art,
Could twist the sinews of thy heart?
And when thy heart began to beat,
What dread hand? and what dread feet?

What the hammer? what the chain?
In what furnace was thy brain?
What the anvil? what dread grasp
Dare its deadly terrors clasp?

When the stars threw down their spears,
And water'd heaven with their tears,
Did he smile his work to see?
Did he who made the Lamb make thee?

Tiger! Tiger! burning bright
In the forests of the night,
What immortal hand or eye,
Dare frame thy fearful symmetry?

THE CLOD AND THE PEBBLE

" Love seeketh not itself to please,
Nor for itself hath any care,
But for another gives its ease,
And builds a Heaven in Hell's despair."

So sung a little Clod of Clay,
Trodden with the cattle's feet,
But a Pebble of the brook
Warbled out these metres meet :

" Love seeketh only Self to please,
To bind another to its delight,
Joys in another's loss of ease,
And builds a Hell in Heaven's despite."

A DIVINE IMAGE

Cruelty has a human heart,
And Jealousy a human face ;
Terror the human form divine,
And Secrecy the human dress.

The human dress is forgèd iron,
The human form a fiery forge,
The human face a furnace seal'd,
The human heart its hungry gorge.

AUGURIES OF INNOCENCE

To see a World in a grain of sand,
And a Heaven in a wild flower,
Hold Infinity in the palm of your hand,
And Eternity in an hour.
A robin redbreast in a cage
Puts all Heaven in a rage.
A dove-house fill'd with doves and pigeons
Shudders Hell thro' all its regions.

A dog starv'd at his master's gate
Predicts the ruin of the State.
A horse misus'd upon the road
Calls to Heaven for human blood.
Each outcry of the hunted hare
A fibre from the brain does tear.
A skylark wounded in the wing,
A cherubim does cease to sing.
The game-cock clipt and arm'd for fight
Does the rising sun affright.
Every wolf's and lion's howl
Raises from Hell a Human soul.
The wild deer, wandering here and there,
Keeps the Human soul from care.
The lamb misus'd breeds public strife,
And yet forgives the butcher's knife.
The bat that flits at close of eve
Has left the brain that won't believe.
The owl that calls upon the night
Speaks the unbeliever's fright.
He who shall hurt the little wren
Shall never be belov'd by men.
He who the ox to wrath has mov'd
Shall never be by woman lov'd.
The wanton boy that kills the fly
Shall feel the spider's enmity.
He who torments the chafer's sprite
Weaves a bower in endless night.
The caterpillar on the leaf
Repeats to thee thy mother's grief.
Kill not the moth nor butterfly,
For the Last Judgement draweth nigh.
He who shall train the horse to war
Shall never pass the polar bar. . . .
The soldier, arm'd with sword and gun,
Palsied strikes the summer's sun.
The poor man's farthing is worth more
Than all the gold on Afric's shore.
One mite wrung from the labourer's hands

Shall buy and sell the miser's lands.
Or, if protected from on high,
Does that whole nation sell and buy.
He who mocks the infant's faith
Shall be mock'd in Age and Death.
He who shall teach the child to doubt
The rotting grave shall ne'er get out.
He who respects the infant's faith
Triumphs over Hell and Death.
The child's toys and the old man's reasons
Are the fruits of the two seasons.
The questioner, who sits so sly,
Shall never know how to reply.
He who replies to words of Doubt
Doth put the light of knowledge out.
The strongest poison ever known
Came from Caesar's laurel crown.
Nought can deform the human race
Like to the armour's iron brace.
When gold and gems adorn the plough
To peaceful arts shall Envy bow.
A riddle, or the cricket's cry,
Is to Doubt a fit reply.
The emmet's inch and eagle's mile
Make lame Philosophy to smile.
He who doubts from what he sees
Will ne'er believe, do what you please.
If the Sun and Moon should doubt,
They'd immediately go out.